DEC 20 '07	DATE DUE	
OC 0 8 '12		
MR 2 0 '14		
NO 0 3 '14		
FE 1 1 '15		
IL 2 2 2015		
NO 1 4 '15		
AP 2 8 '16		
AUG 2 0 2018		
SEP 0 4 2018		
JUN 1 9 2019		

SYMBOLS OF
TIBETAN
BUDDHISM

Assouline Publishing
601 West 26th Street,
New York, NY 10001
www.assouline.com

© 2000 Assouline Publishing for the present edition
First published in French by Editions Assouline
Les Symboles du bouddhisme © 1996, 1999 Editions Assouline

Distributed in all countries, excluding France,
Belgium, Luxemburg, USA and Canada,
by Thames and Hudson Ltd (Distributors), London

ISBN: 2 84323 200 7

Translated by Nissin Marshall

Printed in Italy

SYMBOLS OF
TIBETAN
BUDDHISM

FOREWORD BY THE DALAI LAMA

TEXT BY CLAUDE B. LEVENSON
PHOTOGRAPHS BY LAZIZ HAMANI

ASSOULINE

CONTENTS

FOREWORD

THE DALAI LAMA

Tibetan Buddhism is a tradition rich in symbolism. Not only do we have a multiplicity of symbols, but many of them have many layers of meaning. Some of these are simple and others profound, signifying inner values in physcial forms. These symbols help to show the many different levels and aspects of the Dharma. Tibetan Buddhism has so many different symbols that mentioning one or two examples here will hardly do them justice.

The most complex symbolism in Tibetan Buddhism is found in the Tantras. Tantric practice involves visualizing meditational deities, sometimes with many faces and hands and their many-featured mandalas. All of these characteristics and features have profound symbolic value, which unfolds as one progresses in one's practice and meditation. But the core of the Tantrayana Buddhist practice is the immutable union of method and wisdom, the altruistic aspiration for enlightenment and the understanding of suchness, which are symbolized by the *vajra* and bell used in Tantric rituals.

I feel sure that this beautifully presented book, displaying the wealth of symbolism of Tibetan Buddhism, will deepen appreciation of our culture and its distinctive contribution to the world's precious common heritage. I hope it may also inspire readers to lend their support to our effort to keep these traditions alive.

His Holiness the Dalai Lama, 10 May 1996

INTRODUCTION

BUDDHISM, PHILOSOPHY OR RELIGION, WAY OF LIFE OR WAY OF BEING, NEVER CEASES TO INTRIGUE. ITS MANY FACES BEAR witness to the diversity of its paths, and its countless facets may baffle the neophyte. But the essence remains, deeply rooted and common to all seekers after knowledge: a man, anchored in a moment of history, awakened to announce that the attainment of wisdom was within the power of every individual. Metamorphosis is not sudden, nor can it occur overnight. It demands reflection and time, determination and courage. It may take one lifetime or many, but it is possible. The rest is merely a matter of interpretation and direction, the reading of many symbols.

The man who discovered that message was Siddhartha Gautama, born around 550 B.C. in Kapilavastu, on the present border of India and Nepal. Son of the king of the Shakya Clan, he was a contemporary of Lao-Tse and Confucius, of Zarathustra, Plato and Socrates. One day when out riding with his coachman, he encountered in succession an old man, a sick man, a corpse being conveyed to the pyre, and a wandering ascetic. Deciding to seek the cure to these inevitable evils of human existence, the Prince left palace, wife and child to devote himself to this now unavoidable quest. Years of privation and austerity passed

in vain, until the explorer finally shattered the wall of his own ignorance and found the key to his irrepressible search during a long meditation under the sacred tree (*Ficus religiosa*) of Bodh Gaya.

Henceforth Awakened (for ever), the Prince ceaselessly taught the Four Noble Truths of Suffering, of its Source and its End, and of the Means to overcome it. In his monastic wanderings, he brought about many conversions, and his disciples undertook to spread the Good Word. Having become the Buddha (the "Enlightened One" in Sanskrit), the lord of knowledge and of wisdom (*Bodhi*), he died in Kushinagar, at over seventy years old (*circa* 478 B.C.). His disciples declared that he had attained *nirvana*, the supreme liberation or extinction. At this point history ends and story begins – many stories, tales of millions of human beings who, generation after generation, in land after land, have found comfort and guidance in the teachings of the Enlightened One.

The history of Buddhism subsequently assumed many colors as, by word and example, it conquered both geographical space and mankind. Finally the doctrine itself temporarily quit its Indian habitat, banished by the sword of Mohammedan soldiery and its easy absorption by Hinduism, which turned the Buddha into an avatar of Vishnu. Yet taking the great silk route and the tangled trails of Upper Asia, erudite messengers ranged far and wide to spread the Master's words, which flourished as far as the distant isles of Taprobane, Java and Japan. Vigorous branches continued to thrive in the Indo-Chinese and Korean peninsulas, in the mountains of China, and finally scaled the Himalayan ramparts to take root, in the seventh century, on the high plateaux of the country of Böd.

Through these voyages, and the fruit of such exchanges, parallel schools were established in Kashmir and China, their various fortunes depending on the temper of the times. From the great sites of India (Bodh Gaya, Nâlanda and Sarnath) to the splendid stupa of Borobodur in Java, via Anuradhapura and Polonnaruwa in Ceylon, Nara in Japan, the famous caves of Dunhuang and Koue-Lin in China, the lost oasis of Kara-Khoto and the steppes of Serindia – not forgetting the forest monasteries of Siam and Burma, and the former vast monastic cities of Tibet – their heritage and vestiges bear witness to a consummate artistic wealth skillfully adapted to the local context. This also explains the diversity in the expression of common symbols, invariably interpreted to reflect the specific character of those who fashioned them or revered them.

These pages can only address an arbitrary choice of symbols; in their plethora of expressions, it seemed better to examine their lesser known aspects which require a more subtle approach. So why Tibet? Fashions aside, the Roof

of the World has always exerted so strong a fascination that all and everything was ascribed to it, from the best to the worst. Its relative isolation, first deliberate, later imposed from outside, certainly afforded it an enviable calm for the proliferation of philosophical speculations on time and the universe. Yet the price has been exorbitant: a methodically engineered and programmed destruction. Thus the urgency of understanding its symbols to safeguard their message, failing which this civilization could vanish ineluctably.

Mind and matter, space and time, high and low: every set of opposites is susceptible to a hundred explanations, a thousand interpretations, as many variations as the potentialities latent in the human mind. In a world conceived, not as static but as a perpetual state of becoming, where a human being enjoys the privilege and power of self-fulfilment, space becomes a sort of visible time. According to the Buddhist teachings, in their awakedness, the Buddhas of the three times focus on a single point, the present, the past and the future, although the last of these explicitly belongs only to the domain of probability.

"The essence of the teachings does not change," explains the Dalai Lama. "Wherever they are followed, they are applicable. Yet their superficial aspects, certain rituals and ceremonies, do not necessarily fit within new environments. These things change. No-one can predict how time will change matters in a particular place. When Buddhism came to Tibet, there was no-one to dictate exactly how the rites should be practiced. No dogmatic decision was taken, and with the passing years a single tradition was gradually fashioned in its uniqueness. The cultural heritage varies in different countries. And if the essence remains unchanged, the practice of Buddhism differs from one latitude to the next."

It is important to decipher these signs, to seek in them a new pattern of reading, opening up unsuspected prospects. The horizon retreats to adapt to the wide open spaces, stumbling occasionally on questions so bewildering that the Buddha said: "Life is not a problem to be solved, but a reality to be experienced." Farewell conventional wisdom: through images which are so many projections of the mind, questioning must be pursued to its last redoubts, until one walks alone into the light. The symbols are merely markers, wayside indicators.

According to collective memory, the earliest inhabitants of the country of Böd were sons of a monkey and of a rock demoness. They were offspring of not just any primate, however, but of an emanation of the Bodhisattva of Compassion. Nor were they born of just any sorceress, for the demoness was a deity. From such ancestry, the Tibetans have kept their feet solidly planted in the ground and their eyes turned towards the stars. Through nostalgia for a nomadism of the soul, and sometimes an undeniable penchant for fantasy, certain among them have preserved a taste for endless spaces and the deep meaning of the way. This has affected their way of perceiving the world; combining profundity and simplicity, one

of their great sages bluntly summarized the multisecular doctrine in two fundamental precepts: for the Small Vehicle or *Theravada*, the foundation of all practice, "Do not harm others," and for the Great Vehicle or *Mahâyâna*, the basis of meditative reflection, "Help others." For those who wish to venture further, the *Vajrayâna* or *Tantrayâna*, the Diamond Vehicle, leads inevitably to total Enlightenment. A singular feature of Tibetan Buddhism, it is a happy marriage of the teachings of the two previous stages. It is simply a question of time. Total freedom is within the reach of the hand, or of the heart: it springs in the mind of every person, has no limits besides respect for others, and is also the pledge of attainment of being.

In this light, each symbol deciphered, meditated upon and assimilated, is a key to a perpetually evolving universe where memory reaches back to the remotest past and unveils the future potential in each of us. But it is also a solitary path, a path that one person cannot take on behalf of another.

CHAPTER 1

THE WHEEL OF TIME

TEMPORAL CYCLES CADENCING
THE TIMELESS GESTURES OF EVERYDAY LIFE

TIBETANS ANCHOR HUMAN BEINGS IN THEIR PHYSICAL, SPIRITUAL AND UNIVERSAL DIMENSIONS THROUGH THE WHEEL OF TIME. It is created in colored sands for initiations, or represented on embroidered or hand-painted cloth scrolls.

The Wheel of Time is a sumptuous multi-colored diagram of the initiation of the *Kâlachakra*, one of the Vajrayâna's most complete teachings, at once the opening up of the road to knowledge and the path that leads to harmony. This harmony grows out of a subtle resonance between the human body and mind and the outer universe which encapsulates them within its astrological and cosmic dimensions. Yet the Tibetans have done it with their special genius, marrying the ephemeral and the eternal. In the rigorous and complete practice of the *Kâlachakra*, the Himalayan sages glimpse the possibility of attaining Enlightenment in a single lifetime. Hence its complexity.

According to Tenzin Gyatso, the present Dalai Lama and the fourteenth of the line, the symbolism of the Wheel of Time is closely associated with our world and era: "We firmly believe in its ability to reduce tension," he explains, "we feel that it can create peace, peace of mind, and thereby promote peace in the world. Some day, in centuries to come, the Kingdom of Shambala might well reappear in the reality which seems to be our own, and contribute to the overall task we still need to accomplish in this world."

The spiritual leader has himself conferred this great initiation on more than twenty occasions, between 1954, at Lhasa in his native Tibet, and 1995 at Ulan Bator in Mongolia. Among his destinations were Bodh Gaya and Sarnath, the spiritual centers of Buddhism; Rikon in Switzerland; Madison, Wisconsin in the United States; Barcelona in Spain; Leh in Ladakh; and Mungod in southern India. To attend such an initiation – to observe the preparation of the stupa, listen to the teaching, visually penetrate the universe of colors and symbols, survey the sacred cosmogram and banish all else from view, sows the seeds of a forthcoming happy rebirth.

By attuning the human being to the cosmos, the *Kâlachakra* activates the internal and external forces illustrated by the stupa, the medium of meditation and diagram of the universe, with all the associations it engenders. At the heart of the stupa, in the innermost sanctuary of the deity,

Deity of the Kâlachakra
(thangka in private collection).

within the palace of the primordial conscience represented by the blue *vajra*, Kâlachakra symbolizes the moon, while his consort Vishvamata personifies the sun in the form of an orange yellow point. Wisdom and compassion unite here in an embrace in which all contradictions dissolve, a void that harbors all possibilities.

But the Wheel of Time is also the mechanism that regulates the daily calendar based on lunar cycles. It is no surprise to find a dual root, Indian and Chinese, in the calculation of Tibetan time. It appears that Indian influence was preponderant, although the designation of the years preserves a strong Chinese imprint. To distinguish between these two influences, the Indian computation is qualified as "white mathematics," and the Chinese manner as "black mathematics," this latter also overlapping divinatory practices. Almanacs and astrological tables are frequently used in daily life, highlighting the outstanding events of the year.

The days of the week are named after the planets, and form thirty-day months, their names strictly ordinal: first month, second month, etc. Each month begins on the new moon, so that the full moon marks the mid-month. The Tibetan year is thus lunar, and begins on the new moon in February, preceded by a day called *Gutor*, during which one rids oneself of all that was negative in the previous year. The eve of *Lo-Sar* (New Year) is usually spent doing a thorough house- or tent-cleaning.

Both good and bad days are accounted for in everyday activities, the eighth day of the month being dedicated to the Buddha of medicine, the fifteenth to the Buddha Amitâbha, and the thirtieth to Shâkyamuni, the historical Buddha. On these special days, the effects of any action, positive or negative, are multiplied by one hundred. To restore the concordance between the solar and lunar years, a day is simply skipped from time to time, and the necessary adjustments regularly made to avoid inextricable problems.

Twelve animals – mouse, cow, tiger, hare, dragon, snake, horse, sheep, monkey, bird, dog and pig – order the duodecimal cycle, of which five complete repetitions constitute in their turn a sixty-year cycle. To avoid confusion, an element is added to each of these symbols (earth, metal, water, wood, fire), a gender (masculine or feminine), sometimes even a color, which actually corresponds to one of the elements: yellow ocher for earth, white for metal, blue for water, green for wood, and red for fire. Astrological calculations, still practiced in medicine and horoscopy, make extensive use of these data, with an accuracy that our sober dispositions would find astonishing. By way of example, the Tibetan year 2123, of the fire mouse, began on 19 February 1996.

Astrological calendar. Yama, the Lord of Death, holds a disc in which the three poisons, the eight signs of good omen and the twelve signs of the zodiac are concentrically inscribed.

CHAPTER 2

THE WHEEL OF LIFE

EACH INDIVIDUAL IS ATTUNED
TO HIS OWN SPIRITUAL AWARENESS

THE WHEEL OF LIFE IS A VISUAL DEPICTION OF THE VARIOUS STATES OF BEING. IT IS FOUND IN EVERY MONASTERY, USUALLY PAINTED directly on the wall, but also on paper or cloth supports. The Wheel of Life reminds all sentient beings that the supreme aim is ever and always Enlightenment. Ceaselessly reproduced or recreated through the centuries, it has accompanied generations of rough nomads and refined scholars on the many roads of the quest and of devotion, recalling to each person the passing of time and the Four Noble Truths: the existence of suffering, its origin and causes, its ending and the way to achieve this.

Traditionally, the Lord of Death with the wrathful mien, projecting fangs and forehead wreathed in a macabre crown, holds firmly between his powerful arms a large disc in which four concentric circles of codified dimensions are inscribed. Complete with clawlike nails and a tiger's skin of which the tail and hind paws can be seen, this terrifying personage wears rich serpentine jewels. He is thought to personify destiny, what is ordinarily called *karma*, and symbolizes the transient nature of all phenomena.

This existential breviary is best interpreted by starting at the center. The first circle contains the three spiritual poisons responsible for the evils to come: a black pig for ignorance, a green snake for hatred and envy, and a red cock for lust and greed. A second circle surrounds it, half white, half black. Whoever is ensnared by these evil drives takes the path of darkness (*ngan gro' i lam*) which leads to unhappy rebirths and the fires of hell. The others take the path of light (*de gro' i lam*) which leads to better rebirths and to the fields of liberation.

A dozen smaller tableaux, all explicit, make up the outer circle of the great disc. They unfold the steps of human existence, with easily understandable symbols. Starting at the lower left, the old man seeking his path remains in the grip of ignorance, which is a spiritual blindness. Then, continuing clockwise, the potter turning a pot shapes his destiny by his own acts; the monkey leaping from branch to branch refers to the uncontrolled awareness of the ignorant, which must be disciplined in order to be mastered; the coracle and its two passengers represent name and form, or the energies – physical and spiritual – that are inseparable in the stream of life; the five-windowed house of the fifth vignette evokes the

Traditional representation of the cycle of samsâra.

five senses and the faculty of thought, without which there is no perception of the outside world; and the man and woman in intimate union signify contact, the consequence of perception.

Emotions come next. Thus the woman offering drink to the man arouses desire, the symbol of the thirst for life nourished with perceptions. This leads to sensual attachment, the tendency to cling to the object of desire: a man gapes at the fruit of a tree. In the next image, the attractive young woman suggests procreation, new life developing. Next comes the actual birth, a new life. Finally, the last earthly step is sanction by death, and the preparation for rebirth in one of the six worlds that make up our universe.

Between the outer circle of the human seasons and the double white or black road extend the six worlds where the being must be reborn according to his own acts of body, speech and mind. First, in the center of the upper section, is the paradise of the gods (a temporary paradise, fleeting even if it lasts for centuries, because gods also die when they begin to believe in their own immortality), where they listen to the melody that the Buddha plays for them on the lute, without hearing his implicit warning against the vanity of pleasures. Sometimes echoes of distant combats reach them from the neighboring empire of the Titans, who savagely battle to satisfy irrepressible ambitions. Among them, the Buddha bears his sword.

The bottom half contains three spaces where it is unwise to return: ominous places where evil spirits relentlessly multiply torments. On the right,

greedy monsters tortured by thirst and hunger are unable to assuage their desires due to prohibitive physical deformities. Yet their sky is illuminated by a Buddha bearing a casket overflowing with jewels of the mind. Slightly lower down are the infernal regions, where fire and ice punish the guilty for evil deeds perpetrated under the domination of hatred or anger. This nightmarish world is surveyed by an acolyte of the Lord of Death, who measures the weight of each of the actions of his victims. Yet only he who has committed them is the real artisan of his own doom. The Buddha here carries a flame, the flame of hope, because no life in any of these worlds is eternal.

The last lower level, on the left, is populated with animals, slaves of the goodwill of other beings, and here the Buddha attests his presence by a book. Between this animal kingdom and the home of the gods, lies the realm of men in all their diversity. It is the human being who ultimately enjoys the greatest privilege, because, in this infinitely variegated kaleidoscope, he alone can consciously make the choice to lend an ear to the teaching of a begging monk who shows him the way to end suffering. By awaking from his hallucinated dream, he sheds all chains, be they of gold or of iron, but it is he who must walk on the path.

The Dalai Lama starting to mark out a mandala.

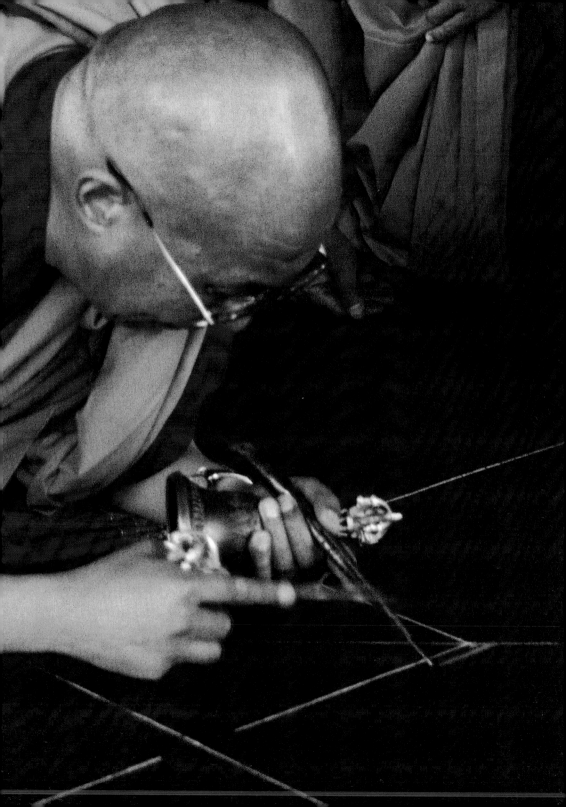

CHAPTER 3

THE WHEEL OF THE LAW

HELP OTHERS, DO NOT HARM THEM

THE WHEEL OF THE LAW IS PRESENT IN EVERY TIBETAN SANCTUARY. IT GENERALLY HAS EIGHT SPOKES, AND IS PICTURED, FLANKED by two gazelles or deer, on the main façade of all monasteries, whether large or small. It symbolizes above all the doctrine preached by the historical Buddha, and the graceful animals that accompany it represent his first two listeners or disciples. Yet Buddhism leaves nothing to chance; behind the apparent simplicity of this first explanation, upon continued reflection, a deeper meaning of the symbol unravels and it must be followed like Ariadne's thread.

The Wheel, or *chakra*, is the endless cycle of birth and rebirth, *samsâra* pullulating with the multitude of beings ensnared in the nets of illusion. The Law as spoken of here is – to be sure – what is implied in its association with "true nature," underlying the natural law of the universe: the ethics and morals of human beings. The supreme truth of the whole diversity of worlds and universes, it was perceived, understood and defined by Prince Siddhartha Shâkyamuni, as the Enlightened One, who formulated it so as to make it intelligible to the generations of the present cosmic cycle.

The eight spokes of the Wheel of the Law symbolize the Eightfold Path, the eight ways of liberation that lead to Enlightenment. The four-spoked wheel evokes the four crucial "moments" in the life of the Buddha, and his disciples considered it an all-conquering weapon to control the passions. It is also the constant reminder of the Four Noble Truths of suffering, its cause, its ending, and the way to achieve this.

According to Tibetan tradition, the Wheel of the Law was set in motion on three occasions: during the first teaching dispensed by the newly enlightened sage in the deer park, near Sarnath; on the appearance of the *Mahâyâna*; and when the *Vajrayâna* or *Tantrayâna* appeared.

The Wheel of the Law also symbolizes the Middle Way. It is the path followed by Shâkyamuni, who warned his followers to shun extremes – rigorous asceticism and unbridled debauchery alike – in order to attain supreme knowledge, which is the fulcrum midway between the reality and the non-reality of things. This shows how important the Wheel of the Law is as a fundamental symbol on which many interpretations are founded, even though these various facets are so many reflections of a single essence.

Classic representation on the façade of a monastery, with the deer emblematic of the first two disciples.

The legend of Siddhartha relates that, after six years of rigorous asceticism, the Buddha in the making replenished his energies with a bowl of rice and undertook to meditate beneath a sacred tree, on the west bank of the Lilajan River (some ten kilometers south of Gayâ, in Magadha), the modern-day Bihar. He had decided not to leave the spot until he had attained Enlightenment, Bodhi. In the course of a famous night, he achieved the goal he had set himself despite the temptations of the legions of Mâra, master of death and of illusion. And the new dawn brought him omniscience.

For seven weeks, Shâkyamuni tasted this unprecedented happiness in the immediate confines, now sacred, of Bodh Gaya. Near the tree of Rajyatana, he met with Tapussa and Balluka, two merchants from the Indian province of Hutkala (modern-day Orissa), who became his first two disciples, and are symbolized by the two animals that accompany the wheel. Some sources claim they are deer, others find gazelles, and yet others insist that they are actually unicorns. . .

The Wheel of the Law, the foundation of human existence, is inseparable from the concept of karma, the act: every act is the fruit of a previous act, bringing a consequence in its wake. This sequence embodies the law of causality. Yet it does not imply a blind or implacable determinism, because, while karma shapes present situations according to previous acts, the individual retains the ability to devise his own response to the conditions of the moment. He has the choice between persisting in the direction conditioned by his past acts, or, on the contrary, taking a path that alleviates his evil tendencies.

Another aspect is that intention generally prevails over actual performance of the act. In the eyes of Buddhists, it is therefore important to avoid any harmful intention, because merely forming the idea gives rise to karmic consequences, good or evil. On the other hand, performed without hatred, without envy or confusion, any act whatsoever remains devoid of karmic results. Acts are physical, but also psychic or verbal: hence the need to preserve the purity of body, mind and speech, which are the bases of an existence according to the law.

The Wheel of the Law stops turning only at the precise moment when the bonds of causality are forever loosened, when the individual is released from illusion and attains the omniscient wisdom of Enlightenment.

Wheel of the Law marked out on a road.

CHAPTER 4

RED HATS
AND YELLOW HATS

UNDER THE PROTECTIVE WING OF THE THREE JEWELS

THE HAT, AN ATTRIBUTE OF CERTAIN RITES, HAS BECOME THE EMBLEMATIC SIGN OF THE SO-CALLED SCHOOLS OF THE ANCIENTS (RED) and the Moderns (yellow).

As Buddhist doctrine evolved locally, four main orders emerged in the Tibetan Land of the Snows. After a first wave of translation of the founding texts, the seventh century witnessed the birth of the Nyingma school, whose adepts are generally called the Ancients and claim the heritage of the sage Padmasambhava.

After the bloody political religious conflicts in later centuries, almost annihilating the Good Law and restoring earlier beliefs, the renewed flourishing of the doctrine gave birth to the Sakya and Kagyü schools. Other currents blossomed in turn around spiritual masters who based themselves on a personal interpretation of the texts, enriched philosophical reflection and trained their disciples in the exercise of particular paths of access to Enlightenment.

Forming and disbanding in a random pattern, often rooted in a remote spot due to the local presence of a hermit or an ascetic, certain minor orders lasted the space of a human lifetime

Eighteenth-century statue representing Tsongkhapa, reformer and founder of the school of "Those who practice virtue."

– the master's. Always more or less sticking to the Eightfold Path, others survived and spread along the byways. Such were the Kagyü order, which had many avatars, and the Kadampa school, originally associated with the Reting Monastery, the influence of which persisted in the Gelug order.

A final wave on the colorful scene of Tibetan Buddhism, the school of "those who practice virtue," owed its birth to the great erudite reformer Tsongkhapa, who founded the famous Ganden Monastery in 1409, after having powerfully contributed to the creation of two other monasteriess, Sera and Drepung. These three great monastic universities are in fact still considered as the "three pillars of Tibet." The Gelugpa, the vehicle of transmission of knowledge and wisdom generated by the reform of Tsongkhapa, ultimately prevailed over the others (Nyingmapa, Sakyapa and Kagyüpa) chiefly through the political ascendancy of the Dalai Lama.

It is nevertheless important to discard the impression of a perpetual antagonism between these different orders. Undoubtedly conflicts occasionally arose between them, due to personal rivalries and diverging interests, often inspired by temporary outside allies. In terms of doctrine, however, Red Hats and Yellow Hats acknowledge each other as faithful servants of the Law of the Buddha. Besides, while the former are associated with the Ancients and the latter are closer to the Gelug order, either hat is sometimes used for specific rituals.

The first indispensable step for the Buddhists of the Land of the Snows is an unreserved commitment to the way, implied by *kyab-dro*, that is to say "seeking refuge" in the Triple Gem. For Tibetan Buddhists, this is a normal prerequisite to any initiation into the Good Law, inasmuch as concrete practice is indissociable from text learning. And besides, to perform meditation exercises correctly, it is necessary to have a master able to direct this dual apprenticeship.

From this requirement stems another, the mutual and judicious choice that seals the relationship between master and disciple. Wherever it may be, the foundation of the Buddhist vision remains the Triple Gem or the Three Gems, which are the Buddha (the Enlightened One), his teaching (the *Dharma* or the Law), and the monastic community (the *sangha*). With the evolution of the *Mahâyâna*, which advanced the notion of the universality of Buddhahood beyond the historical personality of Shakyâmuni, the development of the *Vajrayâna* enhanced the preeminence of the master/teacher who incarnated its principle while living among men. Moreover, the term "lama" is not employed for each and every monk, but is a title reserved for the most accomplished and the most scholarly, sages authorized to teach doctrine and to perform rites, to train others and to guide them to

Enlightenment in accordance with their own aptitudes.

For the strict practitioner, the *Tantrayâna* tradition is to place one's whole existence under the complementary yet capital protection of the "Three Roots": the lama, the source of benediction during the quest; a meditation or tutelary deity (*yidam*), as a token of accomplishment; and the protectors of the Law and the female deities (*dâkinî*), the pledge of enlightened activity. The "taking of refuge" is generally accompanied by prostrations, the physical expression of humility, which is also a way of honoring the teaching.

Monks during a religious service.

26

CHAPTER 5

THE STUPA

A MATERIALIZATION OF THE INTERIOR QUEST

THE STUPA IS A MONUMENT OF INDIAN AND PRE-BUDDHIST ORIGIN, PRIMARILY INTENDED TO MARK THE IMPORTANT PLACES OF THE doctrine consecrated by the historical Buddha's passage on earth: in Lumbini, the village of his birth; in Bodh Gaya where meditation opened the doors to Enlightenment; in Sarnath where he gave his first teaching. A stupa also stands at Kushinagar, to accommodate the Buddha's mortal remains after his physical departure from the land of man (his *parinirvana*).

Adjusting to the vagaries of Buddhist doctrine, the stupa went through many metamorphoses in different latitudes: in Ceylon it became the *dagoba*, in Siam the *chedi*, and in Tibet the *chörten*. Examples both admirable and varied are found in the Royal Singhalese cities, in the sumptuous Shwedagon pagoda in Rangoon, not to mention the marvel of Borobodur in Java, and the countless *chörten* disseminated in the sanctuaries along the pilgrim trails in Tibet.

The perfect proportions of the Buddha's body served as a model for the erection of these distinctive monuments, which were built according to strictly defined rules. The foundation stands on a square base denoting the earth, surmounted by a dome symbolizing water, prolonged by a flight of stairs betokening the steps of Enlightenment and representing fire. A stylized umbrella, emblem of the wind, caps the overall structure and culminates in a crescent moon on which the solar disc rests, the expression of the cosmic supremacy of the Buddhist Law.

In the *chörten*, which frequently serves as a receptacle for offerings or a tomb for great spiritual masters, the Tibetans see the figuration of the body, speech and mind of the Buddha. Architectural variants sometimes include a five-petalled lotus flower crowning the parasol and symbolizing the five lines of Buddhas in the *Mahâyâna*. Other interpretations embody the high points in the spiritual quest, occasionally with the statue of a deity at the center of the reliquary.

Small or large, the *chörten*, or stupa, built amid sanctuaries or standing alone among the mountains, is honored by the faithful, who donate offerings, prostrate themselves before it, burn incense and circumambulate it in a sunwise direction. Alone, in groups or in series, *chörten* always imply the presence of the Buddha, and are indissociable from the reading of the world given by Tibetan tradition.

At Bodnath (Katmandu), one of the best-known relics of the Buddhist world.

CHAPTER 6

THE PRAYER WHEEL

PRAYER FOR THE BENEFIT OF ALL BEINGS

IN A "COUNTRY OF SHEPHERDS AND MONKS, ISOLATED FROM THE WORLD AND SO CLOSE TO THE SKY," OF WHICH JACQUES BACOT SAID at the turn of the century that "the natural occupation of its inhabitants is prayer," the *khorten*, commonly called the "prayer wheel," is undoubtedly the Buddhist ritual object best known to the profane, as well as being the pilgrim's dearest companion. Another name for it is the *chos-kor*, which means "to turn the doctrine" and refers to the first teaching of the Buddha, when he set the Wheel of the Law in motion.

From the smallest to the largest, the prayer wheel always consists of a hollow cylindrical body, usually of metal, engraved with mystic emblems or prayers. It is penetrated along its axis by a rod provided with a handle, if portable, or with two clips if it is fixed to a stand. This applies to all those placed at hand height, along the outer walls of sanctuaries.

Enclosed in the *chos-kor* are sacred texts or invocations (mantra), written on paper or parchment. The cylinder of the wheel is rotated in the same direction as the sun, and each turn is the equivalent of a reading of the prayers enclosed within. Set in motion, the wheel emits a gentle ticking sound in pace with the walker's rhythm.

According to the faithful, this attests to the flight of the prayers thus scattered to the four winds. The portable prayer wheel is fitted with a ball at the end of a small chain fixed midway along the metal body; with a flick of the wrist, the person carrying the wheel sets its twirling rhythm.

Many materials can be shaped to form the body of this singular instrument, not only coarse metal, but also more precious alloys, sometimes even enhanced with mother of pearl, coral or turquoise. Thus certain prayer wheels are genuine works of art.

At the monastery entrance, the *chos-kor* may be of impressive size, protected from the weather by a roof, or even installed in a sort of watchtower with a door. An unencumbered space is provided all around to enable the devotee to accompany the turning wheel which is adorned with sacred mantra. It is driven by one or more handles, which serve to turn the wheel. In the greener lands of the Himalayan valleys, nestled in the faults of the mountain ramparts, a rudimentary but highly effective system is used to harness waterfalls and running streams to turn the prayer paddle wheels, which ceaselessly give voice to

The prayer wheel ceaselessly cadences the pilgrim's path.

pious murmurs, cadencing and echoing with an incantatory and rhythmic regularity.

Tibetans also have a custom of erecting prayer flags, mounted in garlands, on the roofs of their houses, or in the case of nomadic shepherds, on top of their tents. Prayer flags ornament the bridges that straddle torrential streams and they accumulate at mountain passes. These beneficial formulas are printed on small pieces of cloth in the five basic colors (yellow, white, red, green and blue), which stand for the five elements (earth, water, fire, air and ether), the five senses, and the five wisdoms. Prayer flags are a means of spreading the good word to all beings, both in populated regions and in the vastness of deserted spaces. But their function is also to attract good luck, to preserve health by warding off disease, the evil eye, demons and evil spells, and finally, to manifest one's gratitude for a wish fulfilled or an unexpected beneficial occurence.

Near monasteries, prayer flags become victory banners. Mounted on tall poles, they indicate places worthy of attention. They mark the location of sacred caves, and the high points of mountain passes, where the traveler may thank the gods for their protection.

At sowing time, these small colored cloths are placed on the foreheads of farm animals, to ensure good harvests. The yaks that accompany pilgrims also wear them, which serves as a signal that they are not to be sacrificed but should be allowed to die a natural death.

In the middle of the most common model of prayer flag stands the *lungta*, or wind-horse, the bearer of the precious Wish-fulfilling Jewel. It can be inscribed with the name of the person for whom the wind-borne wishes are intended. The remaining space is filled with sacred or magical formulas, and the four corners usually contain a tiger, a lion, a dragon and the mythical bird, the *garuda*. All these animals are symbolic of power and energy. A victory pole can be mounted or garlands of prayer banners assembled for ceremonial occasions: the presence of monks then confers a sacred character on the act, which becomes commensurately more beneficial by being part of a ritual.

Prayer banners.

CHAPTER 7

SACRED MANTRA

"OM MANI PEME HUNG"

THIS MILLENNIAL LITANY IS BOTH THE SYM-
BOL OF BUDDHIST LIFE IN TIBET AND THE
EXPRESSION OF A WAY OF BEING. IT HAS BEEN
the subject of hundreds of exegeses, of thousands
of interpretations. The Tibetans pronounce it *om
mani peme hung*, and its simplest translation would
be "om jewel of the lotus om." For the common
believer, its incantatory recitation suffices to
ensure his spiritual well-being. For the advanced
adept, the complexity of the successive layers of
meaning of each of the sounds, taken individually
or as a whole, unveils the thousand and eight
facets of reality – or illusion. The origin of this
mantra is associated with Chenresig-
Avalokiteshvara, the Great Compassionate One.
He is the supreme Protector of Tibet, and is incarnated in the Dalai Lama, who thereby remains
the spiritual and temporal leader against all comers.

For the *Vajrayâna* or *Tantrayâna* practitioner, the first and last syllables are believed to be
charged with power, and must be handled with
infinite precaution. *Om* is the body, the speech
and the mind of the disciple, at the same time as
those of a Buddha: it symbolizes their metamorphosis, or the attainment of Enlightenment.
Mani, the Jewel proper, grants all wishes and signifies the supreme goal to which one aspires.

Peme, the lotus flower, embodies wisdom, particularly that of the perfect void. And *hung* expresses
the indivisibility, the indissociable unity of
method and wisdom.

Roughly speaking, the Great Tibetan
Mantra states that the practice of a way, by the
inseparable union of wisdom and appropriate
means, can serve to transform a common body,
speech and mind into the perfectly pure equiva-
lence of a Buddha: a whole program of life based
on discipline and reflection, pushed to absolute
limits, until the attainment of full Enlightenment.

Everywhere in the Land of the Snows, the
presence of the Great Mantra is proclaimed on
prayer flags, engraved on roadside stones, or
inscribed on the mountainsides in monumental
displays. It is found on scraps of paper pinned
onto the doors of homes and monastery thresholds; or woven into *khata*, traditional scarves of
praise and happiness. All of Tibet is embodied in
these few words that ring out from moment to
moment, from one life to the next. The Great
Mantra is the land's favorite protector, replete with
inner meaning. Inextricably associated with the
Dalai Lama, it is the most powerful of all utterances.

OM MANI PEME HUNG, *here engraved on a
roadside stone in the five symbolic colors.*

THE ROSARY

THE MÂLA

THE MÂLA IS A ROSARY IN THE BUDDHIST MANNER, ONE OF THE ESSENTIAL ATTRIBUTES OF THE PILGRIM AND OF MANY DEITIES. It has 108 beads, and is used to recite prayers, but, above all, to count the number of repetitions of a particular formula, intoned to a select deity. According to the school and deity, and according to whether the faithful are monks or laymen, they generally keep to the deity to whom they feel closest, to the mantra which they received during a particular initiation, or to the invocation indicated by a lama for a precise purpose, such as protection, cure or gratitude.

The *mani* happens to enjoy the greatest favor. A widespread practice, which may be individual or collective, is to repeat this mantra a million times, for purification, or to increase one's merits. The exercise also helps to calm and clarify one's thoughts, which is the indispensable preparatory phase for meditation.

When the *mâla* is used to intone the recitation, the right hand tells the beads. At rest, it is usually worn as a bracelet, wound around the left wrist. Since Tibetan believers are not at all intimidated by the most astronomical figures, nor put off by the incantatory intonation of the same formula, to avoid getting lost in their counting,

they insert four markers called *chaturmaharâjâ* between the beads of the *mâla*. These are larger beads, or symbolic double pendants (thunderbolt scepter and bell), attached to the body of the *mâla* by a twist of red strings. Ten small rings, mobile or fixed, are threaded above each charm to make counting easier. Tibetan *mâla* normally terminate in three larger beads, which represent the Three Jewels.

Mâla are most commonly made of wood, but can be made of any material, including seeds, glass, precious or semi-precious stones, ivory, jade, coral, turquoise, and mother of pearl. The beads vary in size, but are designed for ease of handling. Color is also important: those who have the means often prefer a color directly associated with a particular divinity for their devotions.

For certain secret rites, Tantric masters formerly used chaplets composed of beads carved out of bone, sometimes even – it is alleged – out of 108 skulls. This was seen as a proclamation on the part of the initiate of his mastery of fear, if not the enigma of death. The *mâla* is also the distinctive sign of famous teachers and of certain divine manifestations.

With its 108 beads, here made of sculpted bone, the mâla *is widely used in Tantric rituals.*

CHAPTER 9

THE ALTAR

NOTHING IS TOO BEAUTIFUL FOR THE ENLIGHTENED ONE

FOR HOME AND SANCTUARY ALTARS ALIKE, THE FOUR IMAGES THAT ARE INDISPENSABLE TO THE BELIEVER IN HIS DAILY PRACTICE ARE usually present: a representation of the Buddha, whether sculpted or painted, accompanied by Avalokiteshvara, the Great Compassionate One, Târâ, the incarnation of the Buddha's activities, and Achala, the deity who removes obstacles. To these basic emblems other deities may be added, objects of personal devotion, the Bodhisattva of loving benevolence, or Maitreya. A sacred text, or sometimes a miniature stupa, symbolizes the word of the Buddha.

Offerings are placed before these emblems: food, fruit and flowers; clear water in the seven ritual bowls; and light shed by candles placed in small dishes. As modest as they may be, the offerings must be prepared with the greatest possible care, and presented with the best intentions. This instruction is without exception, because, if not respected, even the finest things lose their value.

The Dalai Lama repeatedly says "Do not pay too much attention to external things, the accent must be placed more on interior development." It must never be forgotten that the intention behind the offering is even more important than the gesture itself.

Still today, despite destruction, vandalism and theft, the altars of Buddhist sanctuaries display a joyful mélange of objects: small coins, or miscellaneous ritual objects of gold or silver set off with gemstones. A vast range of items can be found laid down in front of the deities: ewers for nectar or lustral water, fans of peacock feathers, crafted conch shells, pairs of thunderbolt scepters and bells (vajra and drilbu), magic daggers (phurba), miniature wheels, mâla, cintamani (the wish-fulfilling jewel, which represents knowledge and the liberated mind), flower vases, fly whisks, three-dimensional mandala, mirrors, swords, spears and tridents, axes and choppers (defensive weapons that protect the Buddha and his Law, as well as the sign of victory over the forces of evil or ignorance).

Ex-votos are offered beneath brocades and thangka. Between these laid-out riches and the penury of the ascetics of bygone ages, are these words of the Dalai Lama: "People like us depend so much on external things, like having statues, incense, butter, lamps and so forth; but if these things bring about no effect in the mind, they are not much help."

The altars of the Tibetan version of Buddhism are often distinguished by abundant decoration.

CHAPTER 10

MUSICAL INSTRUMENTS

AT THE SERVICE OF THE GODS FOR THE BENEFIT OF BEINGS

MUSIC AND SONG PLAY AN IMPORTANT ROLE IN TIBETAN DAILY LIFE, ACCOMPANYING WORK IN THE FIELDS, AS WELL AS DANCE AND entertainment. Formerly the warm season was the occasion for picnics at the water's edge, and Lhasa once had a theater and opera season.

Like all traditional art of the Land of the Snows, music is essentially religious. Dance itself is strongly marked by the influence of the *cham*, or sacred dance of monastic origin. Tibetan liturgical music is rich in fascinating sonorities, where unsuspected echoes can be perceived, and it is said to engender awe. In the most rigorous sense of the term, these sonorities were constructed to foster receptiveness to singular vibrations, a door opening onto a reality beyond reality.

Tibetan sound masters enjoy the reputation of having used the human voice to achieve a rare and profound skill demanding years of pratice, in which exercise is treated as a veritable yoga. According to expert practitioners of this art, it contains, amplified and magnified, the interior melody of the human body, which can be heard by stopping the ears to shut off outside noises. It is a music of transition, of uncommon strength and purity, expressing at once suffering and compassion, a tireless quest and a soothing serenity.

Many wind and percussion instruments also lend their support to this ritual. Perhaps the most impressive of these is the *radong*, a telescopic horn requiring one player, and several carriers. Made of three tapering sections fitted one into the other, it can be as much as fifteen feet long. Usually constructed out of repoussé metal, it is lined with wood in places, and often very skillfully decorated. This horn, with its extremely low-pitched sound, is used to announce the start of ceremonies or to inaugurate public festivities. It is played in pairs, so as to keep the sound continuous, and when in use, its bell-shaped mouth rests on the ground, on a stand, or even on the shoulders of sturdy monks. For the sound to resonate in all its fullness, the musicians are generally positioned on the monastery roof.

The *gyaling*, similar to the oboe, is present in nearly all ceremonies, except for rituals of exorcism. It provides the high notes of the melody and is often richly ornamented. The conch shell is also very popular, its mouthpiece usually silver-plated and its mouth decorated with a cloth pendant. It reminds the faithful of their daily duties but is also used for emergency calls; in the east of

The damaru, *the ritual drum with swinging beads.*

the country, for example, it is used to warn of an approaching hailstorm or blizzard. During certain rites, the initiation of the *Kâlachakra*, for instance, the conch shell is used to distribute lustral water to the participants.

A special ritual trumpet, the *kangling*, normally holds the attention: it is made from a human thighbone, or otherwise a similar animal bone, polished and sometimes artistically crafted. It seems to have emerged in Tibet for the performance of esoteric rites, in the footsteps of the great Tantric masters, such as Padmasambhava (eighth century). It is also often found among the distinctive attributes of the wrathful deities.

Cymbals of various sizes are employed during the services, the largest in the worship of the "wrathful" deities, and the smallest for the benevolent ones, the presentation of offerings, or certain Tantric ceremonies. Their desired sonority is determined by the proportions of metal alloy from which they are made.

The large prayer drum is carried on a single pole stand and struck to measure the rhythm of the procession or ceremony, by means of a long rod curved at the end and fitted with a leather or cloth ball. The monks use it to assemble the community or for Tantric services.

The omnipresent *damaru*, native to India, is a tambourine made up of two wooden hemispheres joined back to back and covered with cloth or leather, each one provided with a small ball at the end of a cord. The rotation of the wrist that holds the handle produces the instrument's characteristic sound. Tantric masters sometimes prefer an object made of two half-skulls, set with precious stones. The *damaru* cadences the mantric recitations or stresses their important passages. The combined sounds of the *damaru*, the ritual bell (*drilbu*) and a bone trumpet are used to invoke rain.

Other instruments are also found in the Land of the Snows: the yak horn is used by magicians and sundry casters of spells, always feared by the populace. In their travels, wandering musicians and bards are often accompanied by a rudimentary lute with one or two strings, probably of Chinese origin.

Musical skills and the difficulties of their apprenticeship have never been the subject of any rigorous transcription, and they are learned in performance. The only indications given are in the form of lines, more or less dense or fine, with the peaks marking fortissimo, and the hollows representing piano.

Preceding double page: novices practicing on the telescopic horn.
Opposite: the cymbal punctuates the prayers during ceremonies.

CHAPTER 11

THE SACRED SCARF

THE *KHATA*

THE *KHATA* IS, FIRST OF ALL, THE SIGN OF A SIMPLE CIVILITY, A GESTURE OF OFFERING, OF WELCOME AND OF COURTEOUS EXCHANGE. IT is present in all ceremonies, large and small, public and private. It is usually white, sometimes orange or golden yellow, and sky blue in Mongolia.

Since Tibetans are well known for their pragmatism and for a subtlety bordering on perversity, the giving of the *khata* obeys a code that is richer in meanings than may first be apparent. In a society where etiquette has always been important – to the point where it was formerly possible to ascertain a person's precise rank from the level of the rugs on which he was posed – the ritual of the *khata* casts a special light.

The handsomest scarves are made of the finest silk, supple and fluffy, slightly moiré, with long fringes. The sacred formula of the *mani* and eight auspicious symbols are woven into the fabric. This *khata* is a substantial piece of cloth, about four yards long and nearly one yard wide, and is nearly exclusively reserved for the highest religious dignitaries and important figureheads. The *khata* of the affluent, though slightly less sumptuous and more widespread, are still made of silk, but are smaller in size (less than three yards long and one yard wide). The most common

scarves are smaller again, and are symbolic more than anything else. Today they are rarely made of silk but instead, when possible, of quality lightweight cotton, but more often of some synthetic material: they have become merely the symbol of a symbol. Nevertheless, *khata* continue to pile up with the same fervor at the feet of the divine effigies, attesting to the vigor of the faith.

The exchange of the *khata* is governed by a code. In the higher ranks of the hierarchy, for a Grand Lama or a high civil dignitary, for example, the scarf is given with the hands joined at the level of the forehead, with a ceremonious inclination of the upper body. This gesture is a testimony of respect and good intentions. If the *khata* is given back, its owner keeps it all the more preciously, because henceforth it becomes the bearer of benedictions, like a talisman. If the interlocutor offers another scarf in return, it is considered as a token of protection, accompanied also by auspicious wishes.

A white, silk scarf, the khata *represents the purity of the gesture, and the respect of the person who offers it.*

CHAPTER 12

THUNDERBOLT SCEPTER AND BELL

DORJE AND *DRILBU*
MEANS AND WISDOM

THUNDERBOLT SCEPTER AND BELL, *VAJRA* AND *GHANTA*, *DORJE* AND *DRILBU*, ARE THE MOST FREQUENTLY ENCOUNTERED OBJECTS ON THE Diamond Path (*Vajrayâna*). Together they represent both the most ordinary and the most complex symbol of Tibetan Buddhism. Whether present in solitary meditation or in the vast gatherings that mark monastic life, their role is essential; without them rites and ceremonies are hardly conceivable.

Unified, they form a symbol which is associated with the incorruptible purity of the diamond, with the truth that no force, no weapon can destroy. Simultaneously, but in another register, they represent the victory of knowledge over ignorance, the mastery of spirit over the "poisons" that tarnish existence.

The thunderbolt scepter, held in the practitioner's right hand, is a token of stability of the method, while the bell, in his left hand, is a reminder of the wisdom of impermanence. Equilibrium between the two is established through ritual gestures, the *mûdrâ*. In the hands of the masters of esoteric interpretation, this inseparable pair signifies the unity of masculine power and of feminine energy, or the emblem of the dual unity of absolute and relative truths.

The *vajra* originally stood for lightning, and is the attribute of the Hindu god Indra. Having been adopted and adapted by Buddhism, in reaching Tibet and becoming the *dorje*, it assumed a dominant place among Tantric symbols. Of metal or of stone, with one to nine points, the commonest thunderbolt scepter generally has three, representing the Three Jewels. With a single double point, the *dorje* stands for the union of the spiritual and material worlds; with two double points (seldom seen), the duality of appearances; with four double points it is associated with the great moments in the life of Çâkyamuni; five points make it a crown; and four points around a shaft symbolize the five elements, the five wisdoms, the five primordial Buddhas. Thunderbolts with nine double points are exceptional, even in Tibet, and are linked to secret interpretations. In all forms, it is a symbol of the absolute beyond all opposites, or of the fundamental unity achieved by meditation.

The double *dorje*, or intersected *vajra*, is sometimes interpreted as the Wheel of the Good Law. Consisting of two thunderbolt scepters joined at the center, it denotes the indestructibility

An essential symbol, dorje and drilbu express the indissoluble alliance of method and wisdom.

of the essence of all phenomena, the most complete understanding of the adamantine truth.

The *dorje* very often adorns the handle of the bell, of which it is the pendant, a sign that their functions are indissociable in daily practice. The prototype of this emblem par excellence of Tibetan Buddhism is closely guarded at the Sera Monastery on the outskirts of Lhasa. It is accessible to the public only once each year, on the occasion of a major ceremony. It is thought to have belonged to Padmasambhava himself, and was found in his meditation cave at Yerpa by his disciple Dacharpa.

The bell, *ghanta* or *drilbu*, is at once the opposite and complement in this symbol of transcendental knowledge. Its handle may terminate in a stupa, a *cintamani*, or a single- or many-pointed *dorje*. It represents not only sound, but also void and impermanence: its crystal tinkle dies no sooner than emitted, recalling that all is fleeting. It is thus the symbol of the immediate wisdom of intuition, which instantly grasps and understands the void without reflection or reasoning. Endowed with creative power by the attendant vibration of the mantra or *dhârani* which it accompanies, the ritual bell also has the function of inspiring and activating the enlightenment of the heart.

In a world ruled by opposites, where there is no day without night, no nadir without zenith, no north without south, no sunrise without sunset, the symbolic pair *dorje* and *drilbu* mirrors the image of interdependent opposites, indissolubly united: it is the original essence of the Diamond Path, the seed of the double unity of contradictory appearances through which it is manifested. In this sense, the diamond scepter expresses the perfect clarity of the void, veiled by the endless diversity of its masks. For the needs of certain rituals, *vajra* and *ghanta* represent the two fundamental diagrams, virtually inseparable in the Buddhist universe, which are the stupa of Garbhadhâtu and of Vajradhâtu, or the world of appearances and the world of spiritual energies and forces. The combination of these two aspects is always indispensable for the attainment of Enlightenment.

Monk during a service with thunderbolt scepter and bell.

RITUAL BOWL AND DAGGER

TRIUMPH OVER INTERIOR ENEMIES

THIS IS PERHAPS ONE OF THE MOST STRIK-ING PARADOXES OF THE TIBETAN WAY OF BUDDHISM: ON THE ONE HAND, THE MASTERS and practitioners owe their universal reputation to their peaceful strength, to the quality of their listening, and to their serenity – and, on the other, representations of fierce, wrathful and terrible deities abound, at first inspiring a feeling of repulsion, rejection, and even fear. It must be borne in mind, however, that these allegories are merely other facets of the benevolent and protective deities, projections of the mind, one of the functions of which is to fight the enemies of the doctrine, while also, by transmuting them, to annihilate the spiritual "poisons" that pose obstacles to Enlightenment. Thus these fearsome effigies are accordingly furnished with weapons of all sorts, and these are freely used by the adepts of Tantrism in their practices.

Three objects from this well-stocked arsenal are relatively common. The *kapâla* is a bowl, often mounted on a carefully crafted support, made of a delicately worked skull and fitted with a lid. It is used by the ascetic during secret solitary practices, or during monastic services in honor of the protective deities. In the latter case, it is filled with beer or tea, signifying ambrosia or blood. Its

use is not accorded to all, since it implies authorized transmission. He who employs it must have a clear understanding that it is a reminder of the transient nature of existence.

The *phurbu*, or ritual dagger, was originally a simple nail. Today, it consists of a small triangular blade (usually of metal and sometimes of wood), which is surmounted by a short haft, often in the effigy of a deity or in the form of a *dorje*. Widespread, the *phurbu* is ascribed magical qualities. It is used to keep bad vibrations and diseases at bay, to expel evil spirits, to combat the enemies of the Law, and even to control the clouds in the science of weather-making. The *phurbu's* effectiveness is enhanced when it is used in a trio. Its role is essential to the sacred masked dances and in the sanctuaries of the tutelary divinities, where it may even have its own altar. Joined in a ring, 108 *phurbu* form a protective circle that wards off harmful influences.

The third of the common weapons, the *trigug* (or *kartîka*), is closer to a semi-circular cleaver with a central, solid handle. Its sharp, blade serves to "cleave the bonds of ignorance."

Opposite: ritual cleaver to break the bonds of ignorance.
Following double page: bowl, dagger, and ritual cleaver.

CHAPTER 14

THE AUSPICIOUS SYMBOLS

EIGHT EMBLEMS TO BRING GOOD LUCK AND SECURE PROTECTION

THESE EIGHT EMBLEMS, OR *TASHI TAG GYE*, WHICH ARE OMNIPRESENT IN TIBETAN SPIRITUAL LIFE, ORIGINATED AT A CRUCIAL moment in the life of the historical Buddha. Some say that when the Prince-ascetic finally obtained his goal, in the dawn that followed the famous night under the Tree of Bodh Gaya, joy and gladness spread to all the kingdoms of the universe. And to manifest this great happiness, the celestial beings flocked to the site, loaded with myriad gifts for the Enlightened One. The memory of the centuries and of mankind has retained some of these presents, which were judged essential and became emblematic of the veneration shown to the Master.

These symbols adapt to all fantasies of expression. They may be fashioned into jewels, sculpted in wood, printed on paper or parchment, or even reproduced in simple decorations on everyday objects and ritual instruments. They are found at public and private meetings, at major ceremonies, or when welcoming high-ranking dignitaries. Ascribed the reputation of bringing luck when applied to tents and the thresholds of houses, they appear at the entrance to monasteries and prayer rooms, but are also inscribed on mountainsides and on roadside rocks. On feast days, they are depicted in white or red powder on the paths taken by the guests or processions. They sometimes adorn stupa, and the finest *khata* display them, subtly woven into the silk.

The precious umbrella, *chatra* or *rinchen dug*, is the sign of royal dignity and offers protection from all evils. The two golden fish, *matsya* or *ser-gyi-na*, the insignia of the Indian master of the universe, here express spiritual liberation. They stand for the beings saved from the ocean of suffering of earthly existence. The treasure vase or bowl, *kalasha*, or *bumpa*, contains spiritual jewels, and can serve as a receptacle for lustral water, considered to be the nectar of immortality. The lotus flower, *padma* or *pema*, symbolizes original purity. It is found in various colors and forms, and is a privileged attribute of the Buddhas and Bodhisattvas.

The white conch shell, *sankha* or *dungkar*, which is even more revered if its spiral winds rightward, signifies the word that proclaims the glory of the Enlightened Ones, and sometimes bears the name of victory trumpet. The endless knot, *srivasta* or *pälbeü*, is a token of love or eternity, representing infinite life. The great banner,

Writing on parchment.

56

dhvaja or *gyältsen*, is in fact a wound flag, testifying to the power of Buddhist teaching or the victory of the Good Law. And the golden wheel, *chakra* or *khorlo*, is naturally the wheel of teaching (*Dharma*), to be practiced assiduously to attain Enlightenment. It represents the unity of all things and remains the quintessential symbol of Buddhist doctrine.

In Tibetan tradition, it is not uncommon to associate the eight auspicious emblems with the seven jewels, *saptaratna* or *rinchen nadün*, which are attributes of the *chakravartîn*, or ruler of the world. This mythical personage is impartial and fair, magnanimous and literate, and, like all legendary princes, the protector of widows and orphans. These exceptional qualities are, quite logically, also ascribed to the Buddha.

This indispensable suite to the glory of the universal monarch naturally includes the wheel, *chakra* or *khorlo*; the precious jewel, *ratna* or *norbu*, which grants all wishes, and which is also one of the names given by the faithful to the Dalai Lama; the magnificent queen, *rani* or *tsunm*; the best civil minister, *mantrim* or *lönpo*, a peerless administrator without whom there cannot be a great king; the best white elephant, *hâti* or *langpo*, whose strength is invaluable at the hour of combat; the fastest horse, *ashva* or *tamchog*, who works miracles at festive tournaments and leading troops into battle; and the best of military commanders, *senapati* or *magpon rinchen*, to pre-

serve the empire. An eighth emblematic personage is sometimes added to these seven royal insignias: the best great treasurer, *khyimdag*, who holds the purse strings in complete justice and ensures the well-being of the sovereign's subjects.

The eight auspicious symbols and the seven jewels, which are extremely popular and widespread, may appear alone or in groups, or even in a random order, as dictated by the needs of the moment. At special events, such as weddings, the eight auspicious emblems are united into a single composition, called *tag gye pünzog*, rich in all the meanings which they convey.

Four of the eight auspicious signs: the Wheel of the Law, the endless knot, the royal parasol and the jewel cup.

CHAPTER 15

OFFERINGS

SACRED AND PROFANE OFFERINGS,
A HOMAGE TO THE DEITY

THE OFFERING, AN INTEGRAL PART OF MEDI-
TATION AND LITURGY, IS ALWAYS A GESTURE
TO THE DEITY: HUMILITY, PRAISE, OBEDIENCE,
prayer or gratitude. It is a sort of direct relationship betokening the respect or devotion of the
faithful. Offerings of light and water are the most
common: a lamp burns permanently on every
Tibetan altar. Legend has it that the Precious
Master himself, Padmasambhava, declared more
than twelve centuries ago that the water of the
Land of the Snows was so clear that it was pure
enough even for the gods.

These do not necessarily, however, satisfy
the faithful, who swell their gifts with money,
incense, flowers and fruit, *khata*, as well as cakes
prepared explicitly for the purpose. These include
torma and *tsog*. The former are made on the spot,
in the courtyard of the sanctuary or on the parvis,
with *tsampa* (barley flour, the Tibetan staple) and
butter. Monks and laity usually partake in the
operation, which is conducted with vivacity and
good humor. The most skillful then decorate the
traditional shapes in bright colors. These ritual
offerings are placed on the altars to be imbued
with good vibrations, and are then shared among
the participants when the ceremony is over.

Festive offerings, called *tsog*, are more elabo-
rate and intended to be consumed by those who
have prepared them. This once led the Dalai
Lama to say, "When we talk of *tsog*, we think of
something delicious to eat, whereas when we talk
about a ritual cake, we think of something to be
thrown away. This is a mistake. When you make
offerings, you should do it as best you can." The
monks of the Three Pillars of Tibet, namely the
three monasteries of Sera, Drepung and Ganden,
formerly assembled in Lhasa in the second month
of the lunar year (March) for a great meeting of
festive offerings.

At certain ceremonies, the offering may
consist of 108 lamps, 108 bowls of rice, 108 ritual
cakes, and 108 tea bricks. What really counts is
the sacred number. In the olden days, at exceptional festivities, astonishing offerings were prepared, sculpted in butter, and richly decorated,
then proudly displayed by their authors and
admired by spectators. During private meditation,
it is also possible to offer oneself, body, speech
and mind, to the deity.

Bowls of clear water, butter lamps, incense and ritual cakes.

CHAPTER 16

THE SCRIPTURE AND THE TEXTS

TREASURES TO PRESERVE THE MEMORY

WRITING REACHED THE LAND OF THE SNOWS BY ROYAL WILL AND AS PART OF A DELIBER-ATE PLAN TO BECOME INSTRUCTED AND TO instruct. This occured in the time of the great King Songtsen Gampo of the Yarlung dynasty, who unified various principalities into a formidable empire for the first time. History credits him not only with having transferred his capital to Lhasa by leaving the Tsetang Valley, but also for having sired a large family, as two distant princesses, one Nepalese and the second Chinese, arrived to join his three Tibetan wives.

The two beautiful foreigners were pledges of alliance with neighboring courts fearful of the military power of the conquering sovereign. Yet it was based on this dual influence that the monarch adopted the doctrine of the Buddha, and, since that time, despite the hazards and vicissitudes of passing centuries, the Good Law has remained the touchstone of Tibetan civilization.

Around the year 640, the King felt the need to record the teachings which the wandering monks and missionary pilgrims had disseminated for some time through mountains and valleys. However, as the monarch admitted, the Tibetans had hitherto been little concerned with spiritual matters, and notably lacked any means of written expression. Songtsen Gampo accordingly decided to send a group of trusted young men to India, the land of the Buddha, with the specific assignment of studying and bringing back whatever was needed to accord to the royal wish. Among these was Thönmi Sambhota, whose title of Minister promised him a great future.

The trip was not easy, and out of the group of emissaries that bravely departed for Kashmir, at that time the brilliant home of Buddhist thought, fifteen succumbed to the diseases and obstacles on the way. Thönmi Sambhota pulled through, studied assiduously, and returned home armed with sufficient knowledge to construct an alphabet inspired by Sanskrit, and a grammar adapted to the peculiarities of the Tibetan language. Both are still current and offer an uninterrupted view of the evolution of the written tradition, which is essentially religious.

The Tibetan alphabet has twenty-seven consonants and five vowels. While the spoken language has changed throughout the years, the classical written language has hardly been modified at all: capitals are still used in printing (by xylography), while cursive or running hand is

Page from a wood-engraved book.

supplemented by ornamental variants, reserved more specifically for ritual texts.

With these new tools, added to the formula for an indelible ink, also brought back from Kashmir, Tibet witnessed a period of dizzying intellectual effervescence. Indian pandits, assisted by their local pupils, supported by masters and reputed scholars invited to share their knowledge, and actively seconded by outstanding translators, busied themselves for years, indeed centuries, in explaining, interpreting and commenting on the basic texts, brought back from India at such a terrible price. Every monastery had its own library, and many ascetic sages inspired new streams issuing from the same central idea.

Two collections of works, translated from Sanskrit into Tibetan in the course of about six centuries of sustained and exemplary efforts, formed the foundation of this religious literature. The *Kanjur*, in 108 volumes, is composed of the teachings of the historical Buddha as gathered by his disciples, while the *Tanjûr*, in 227 volumes, contains the commentaries on these founding texts. Copied identically by meticulous scribes, they were piously preserved on loose sheets, between wooden boards, enveloped in protective cloths, stacked on hundreds of shelves nestled in chapels, and revered at the same level as statues and other sacred objects. The most precious copies were made by hand, in gold ink.

It needed the destructive folly of the cultural revolution of the twentieth century to scatter, burn and annihilate the main part of this heritage of humanity; the loss is especially tragic because many antique Buddhist treatises had already disappeared elsewhere, especially in India and China, swept away by local historical upheavals. The Tibetan translations were often the last remaining testimony of a wisdom threatened by human folly. Today, it is in the cellars of the Russian museums, the hiding places of the desecrated former sanctuaries of Mongolia, the keepsakes of emigré families and the entrails of the libraries of Europe and America, that the surviving treasures, retrieved by intrepid explorers and coated with the dust of time or oblivion, are exhumed.

Fortunately, the inflexible monastic custom which demanded that the ancient texts be learned by heart has helped save this knowledge from another era, and the texts gathered scrupulously from the monks of the Tibetan diaspora have been set down so that they can be safeguarded for future generations.

Since thousands of Tibetans have been forced to go into exile, even popular songs and traditional epics belonging to a living and eternal oral tradition have been compiled and set down, so that, even under threat, one can be sure that these roots will some day bear fruit again.

Preceding double page: Works kept in a monastic library ; page from a classic work. Opposite: the most precious texts are written in gold ink.

ཉེས་དང་། པས་ཀྱི་ལ་གནེས་གཉ་ ་བྱ། སེམས་སྲོག་ལ་གཔ་བས་ཝེ་བ་ ་
་བ་འི། པས་ཀྱི་ལ་མ་ཕན་ ◯ ་ནི། ར་ལྷ་བས་ཀས་མ་ལ་ཀྱི་དུར་ཀྱ་

༄༅། །མ་ནི་ངལ་ས་མ་ལ་བ་གྱུ་ས་ ་ ་ ་ ་
་དས་ང་ཀུ་ན་དནས་ྱང་ ་ཤ་ག་ ་ ་ ་ ་ ་
་ཞེས་ག་ ་ག་བ་ ་ ་ ་ ་ ་ ་ ་ ་ ་ ་
་པ་ང་མ་ཚ་ ་ ་བཅོག་ཉ་ཨ་གུ་ ་བ་ ་གཔ་ ་
་ ་ ་ ་ ་ ་ ་ ་ ་ ་ ་ ་ ་

CHAPTER 17

MÛDRÂS

SIGNS FOR THE EXPRESSION OF INDESCRIBABLE FORCES

THE WORD ITSELF MEANS "SEAL" OR "SIGN," REVEALING THE INTENTION TO BOTH SEAL AND TO DEMONSTRATE, IN OTHER WORDS TO "translate" words by different means. In short, a species of visual alphabet that serves to attain the essential beyond speech. Here also, the heritage is Hindu, but the interpretation varies with the latitudes, and, as very often in the vast Buddhist panorama, the Tibetan variant has its singularities. These sacred gestures flourished with greater exuberance in the schools of the Great Vehicle, while those of the Small Vehicle generally restricted themselves to the distinctive seals characterizing the rigorously precise and codified "moments" in the life of the Enlightened One.

Among these myriad gestures some are preeminent, in that they permit the immediate identification of an effigy, by associating it with a family or school. They are routinely used in religious ceremonies. The most widespread throughout the Buddhist world is the *anjali mûdrâ*, the hands joined vertically at the height of the breast. Greeting and veneration alike, it is characteristic of the praying figures of certain minor deities, but, above all, it remains, still today, the ideal way to

Gestures to reach beyond words.

greet a person in India, Thailand, Burma and Tibet.

Obviously, the commonest way to pay tribute to the Enlightened One is to join the hands above the head, which is inclined at the same time. Its religious interpretation refers to the cardinal notion in the *Mahâyâna* of the True Nature of all things, of the attainment of Enlightenment which integrates object and subject.

The *dhyâna-mûdrâ* is widely known: the hands one upon the other and resting in the lap of the meditator, palms upward, fingers extended and thumbs touching at the tips to form a triangle, it is a characteristic *mûdrâ* of meditation, of concentration on the *Dharma*. It clearly symbolizes Enlightenment, the privileged moment when opposites are transcended and the road to omniscient wisdom opens. When the personage represented in this posture has a bowl in his hands, the Tibetans refer to him as the Buddha of Medicine.

The gesture of touching the earth, in other words left hand on the knee in the lotus position and right hand downward and turned inward, is the gesture of Çakyamûni at the dawn of Enlightenment: the earth bears witness to his spiritual accomplishment. This is the *bhumisparsha mûdrâ*, found everywhere in the Buddhist geographic area. It also specifically indicates an

unshakable solidity, as personified by the Buddha Akshobhya and the historical Buddha.

The two hands in front of the breast, thumbs and forefingers forming two touching circles, right hand turned outward and left hand either upward or inward, indisputably express the *Dharmachakra*, the setting in motion of the Wheel of the Law. This is naturally the distinctive gesture of Çakyamûni, but also of Maitreya, the Buddha of the Future, and sometimes also of Amitâbha, Buddha of Infinite Light, very popular in all variants of the *Mahâyâna*.

The *vitarka mûdrâ* is the gesture of teaching, or of explanation that convinces: right hand upward, palm outward, left hand downward, also palm outward, with the thumb and forefinger of each forming a circle, thus referring to the perfection of the Buddha's Law. In Tibet, this *mûdrâ* often reversed, is also quite characteristic of the effigies of Târâ and of the Bodhisattvas.

The upright hand, generally the right, at shoulder height, palm opened outward, and the left hand alongside the body, or both hands making the same gesture, offer protection and goodwill, while also indicating the lack of fear: this is the *abhaya mûdrâ*, Çakyamûni's first gesture immediately after Enlightenment. It is mainly found among standing or walking Buddhas, particularly in representations that are common in Southeast Asia. But it is also a gesture of protective power or appeasement, which refers to the need to shed fear in order to advance on the path of knowledge. Amoghasiddhi, one of the five

Great Buddhas, is often depicted in this way.

The *varada mûdrâ* symbolizes welcome, giving, generosity and compassion: right hand turned outward and downward, this gesture is often associated with the *abhaya mûdrâ* of protection and serenity. It denotes the wish to devote oneself to human salvation and to strive to lessen the sufferings of men, so that they may finally attain the perfection of Enlightenment. It is also the reputed seal of the granting of wishes.

Buddhist iconography contains many variants of these *mûdrâ*, generally associated with the recitation of the mantra. During ritual exercises, they induce certain states of mind which help advance on the path of the interior quest. The esoteric schools make considerable use of it, usually strictly codified with respect to a precise Buddha or a particular energy harnessed in the pursuit of a predetermined goal. Some *mûdrâ* must be used with the greatest caution, especially if associated with the propitiation of fierce or wrathful deities, whose formidable powers might be invoked incorrectly by seekers of the absolute incapable of controlling them.

The earth is taken for witness (of Enlightenment) ;
gesture of protection against all forms and aspects of fear.

CHAPTER 18

THE GREAT PRAYER

MONLAM CHENMO
THE ANNUAL INVOCATION FOR THE
WELL-BEING OF BEINGS

THIS CEREMONY IS ASSOCIATED WITH THE NEW YEAR FESTIVITIES. TRADITION ATTRIBUTES ITS CODIFIED INSTITUTION TO Tsongkhapa the reformer, the spiritual father of the youngest school of Tibetan Buddhism (the Gelugpa or Yellow Hats, or, more precisely "those who practice the way of virtue"). With the establishment shortly thereafter, in the sixteenth century, of the line of the Dalai Lama, largely founded on these teachings, political power was the privilege of the adepts of the reformed branch, and of the three great monasteries Ganden, Sera and Drepung, near Lhasa. Created on the impetus of Je Tsongkhapa, they have since then been considered as the "three pillars of Tibet."

Just as everywhere else in the world, the new year has always been the pretext for festivities and revelry, including jousting tournaments among the good-natured Tibetans, who like to indulge their pleasures and rarely forego entertainments. The patronal festivals of the monasteries also provide the opportunity for colorful encounters, marked first by the recitation of epics and performance of sacred dances for two to three days, followed by equally popular profane entertainments.

Custom has it that, on New Year's Eve, everyone should do their housecleaning, to expel the evil spirits and harmful influences due to the faults and negative actions of the previous year. Nomads do likewise in their tents, and whole families set off on pilgrimage to monasteries and sanctuaries, in order to secure solid protection for the coming months. In Lhasa, the capital, it is customary for a scapegoat, generally a vagrant or some unlucky creature, to be loaded with all the evils and solemnly conducted outside the walls, accompanied by a tremendous rolling of drums and blaring of music to dispel all dangers.

In the past, this was also the time when the keys to the city were put into ecclesiastical hands, and throughout the ceremonies and festivities the monks took charge of law and order in the "city of the divine." Honors went to the *dob-dob*, guardians and experts in the martial arts, who were responsible the rest of the year for ensuring compliance with the discipline of daily life in the monastery. About three weeks of the first month of the lunar year (which begins with the new moon in February according to the Gregorian calendar) were devoted to these community activities, marked on the fifteenth day of the month by a public teaching of the Dalai Lama. Special rites

The principal personage of a ritual dance.

74

were performed three times daily in the most venerated sanctuary in Tibet, Jokhang, which houses the statue of the Jo-Wo (an effigy of Çakyamûni preciously guarded in the holy of holies of the temple since the seventh century, when it was brought there by the Chinese wife of the great King Songtsen Gampo). Tens of thousands of monks participated in these ceremonies, and in the weeks marked by alternating prayer and festivity, Lhasa was swollen with a floating population at least three times larger than usual, a crowd as immense as a hundred thousand people according to historical documents.

This tradition is scrupulously observed in exile: Tibetans and neo-Buddhists of Tibetan schools throng each year to Dharamsala, in Himachal Pradesh in India, for the occasion. Dharamsala is where the spiritual leader resides and is the administrative center of a government in exile that strives to address the interests of a small community, scattered chiefly throughout India and in a few other more or less distant countries. For some of the participants, the occasion offers the possibility of replenishing their energies in confirmation of the communal cohesion which unfailingly amazes them, and for all, it is the chance to share precious moments of what may be called communion. In fact, during these always exceptional festivities, the religious and the profane are intimately linked, conferring an unusual vividness to daily activities.

The *Monlam Chenmo* ceremony bears the mark of this fervor. Instituted around 1408, the great prayer for the well-being of all beings perfectly reflects the key idea of the *Mahâyâna* and the ideal of those who travel its path. It was also the biggest monastic gathering in the "city of the divine." This is in fact still true, except for a period of some twenty years, when it was purely and simply prohibited by the Chinese occupation authorities. Although celebrated anew since the eighties, due to the absence of the Dalai Lama, and the surveillance to which it is subjected, it certainly lacks its former luster; this was true even when the ceremony was conducted by the Pänchen Lama, authorized by Beijing to spend a few days among his own.

It was precisely during the preparations for this ritual in 1989 that the second hierarch of Tibetan Buddhism died in circumstances that many Tibetans still consider suspect. The test of strength initiated in 1995 between the Dalai Lama and the Chinese government concerning this succession leaves uncertainties clouding the future and the line of the Pänchen Lama and of the Great Prayer, as formerly known and practiced by generations of Tibetans in Tibet.

Ritual dance mask.

CHAPTER 19

THE MASTERS OF KNOWLEDGE

FROM MAGIC TO PHILOSOPHY,
THE MIDDLE WAY FROM SCIENCE TO KNOWLEDGE

ALTHOUGH IT DID NOT ALL ENTIRELY BEGIN WITH PADMASAMBHAVA, HE NEVERTHELESS STANDS OUT AS THE FOUNDING FIGURE OF Tibetan Buddhism. Responding to a call from Trisong Detsen, on the urging of the philosopher Santarakshita, the great sage came to Tibet to pacify the opposing forces which hindered the consolidation of the Good Law. Born in the semi-mythical kingdom of Orgyen, which some locate in northeastern Kashmir and others in the confines of Bengal, his real existence is nonetheless established, albeit embellished by legend in the intervening centuries. Guru Rimpoche, as he is still named today throughout the Himalayan arc, was a "Precious Master" in many respects.

A century after King Songtsen Gampo had embraced the doctrine of the Buddha, it had steadily advanced, but clashed with the resentment of the supporters of the pre-Buddhist religion of Bön and the persistent power of shamanistic deities. Around 760, Trisong Detsen, grandson of Songtsen Gampo, decided to erect the first Tibetan monastery at Samye, not far from Lhasa, so that Santarakshita, the great Indian wise man who had renounced his position as abbot of the famous University of Nalanda to teach in Tibet, might ordain the first native monks. Operations, however, were hindered, because whatever the men built by day, the genies tore down at night. In the understanding that knowledge and erudition were not sufficient to overcome these harmful influences, Santarakshita advised the king to hand over the task to Padmasambhava, "the Lotus-Born," whose reputation as a highly accomplished yogin and master of the Tantra (esoteric instructions) had spread far and wide.

By harmoniously blending supreme wisdom and extraordinary powers acquired thanks to a peerless native intelligence, inflexibly shaped by rigorous discipline, Padmasambhava soon brought the adversaries of the doctrine to heel. Not content with pacifying them, he made them protective guardians of the Buddhist Law, and unremittingly strove to teach them until the end of his life in Tibet.

Padmasambhava traveled the land to its remotest corners. His many caves of solitary meditation, still piously maintained to our day, dotted the vast expanses of the Tibetan plateau. He is greatly revered, in particular by practitioners of the school of the Ancients, the Nyingmapa.

Eighteenth/nineteenth-century bronze, representing Padmasambhava, one of the key personages of Tibetan Buddhism.

Through the centuries, its adepts have discovered valuable *terma* (hidden treasure texts) which he had carefully concealed here and there, awaiting a time when they might be understood. Gifted with the exceptional powers characteristic of sages, Padmasambhava is also credited with prophesying a number of events which actually occurred later in history.

Padmasambhava is commonly represented in the lotus posture, holding a *dorje* in his right hand and a ritual cup in his left. He is often accompanied by his consort, Princess Mandarava, and his principal feminine disciple, Yeshe Tsogyal, an accomplished yogini, who wrote the master's biography. Mandarava was given to him by her father after a miracle: outraged to find the guru dispensing his teachings to five hundred nuns and to his own daughter, the king of Zahor ordered that the presumptuous sage be burned alive. He changed the fire into a lake of pure water, from which he emerged enthroned on a lotus. The king was so impressed that he immediately adopted the *Dharma* and gave the sage his daughter as a pledge of loyalty. Yeshe Tsogyal was one of the wives of Trisong Detsen before devoting herself to the quest for Enlightenment, which she attained in a single life under the wise direction of Padmasambhava. Some call her "the celestial dancer," considering her a *dâkinî*, an emanation of the inspiring energy of awareness, leading to the perfect understanding of supreme reality.

A face of wisdom.

Among Tibet's other significant figures, Nâgârjuna has a special place. This Indian guru, who lived in the second or third century, and whose name connects him to the *Nâga* who instructed him in their aquatic kingdom, was never actually in Tibet. Yet the philosophical system which he constructed, the *Mâdhyamika*, or middle way, became the cornerstone that led Tsongkhapa to the reform that later gave birth to the school of the Gelugpa. He therefore enjoys special renown and is highly venerated.

The vicissitudes of Tibetan history led Buddhism through many ups and downs. Years of royal protection were followed by periods of destruction, which failed to thwart the renaissance and rooting of the Good Law. After the era of persecution of Langdarma, reconstruction began in Amdo in northeastern Tibet, where a handful of faithful found refuge and succeeded in keeping the tradition alive. They regained the monastery of Samye, settled there, and resumed the broken thread of translations.

Among these faithful and determined intermediaries, Rinchen Zangpo accomplished much that was decisive. To satisfy the desire of the king, who wished to separate the good grain of the *Dharma* from the chaff that the historical upheavals had engendered all around, he set forth to seek one of the wisest of Indian pandits, the high priest of the monastic University of Vikramashila, the master Dipankara Srîjnâna, whom the Tibetans call Atisha, the "great saint." A youth spent in wandering had enabled this

aspirant to wisdom to receive the most diverse teachings available at the time from Râjagriha in Bihar all the way to Orgyen. The Buddha Çakyamûni himself is said to have appeared to Dipamkara in a dream and commanded him to become a monk, which he did, subsequently dispensing the instructions of the Law in Java and Sumatra. Returning to India, he continued his studies and teachings in the great Buddhist universities, ultimately reaching Tibet when more than fifty years old, in the year 1042. After settling in Thôling, he set himself to work with the team of Rinchen Zangpo, translating the basic texts illuminating the doctrine.

Atisha himself wrote many commentaries and sets of instructions, of which the best known, "The Lamp on the Road to Enlightenment," is still authoritative. It is to Atisha that the Tibetans undoubtedly owe their deep attachment to Târâ Drölma, the master's tutelary deity. Her sanctuary near the capital, which also contains the tomb of Atisha, was one of the few to escape the destruction by the Red Guards. Historians consider Atisha to be the founder of the Kadampa (oral teaching) school, which stressed the intense practice of meditation to release the spirit from the impurities that plunge it into darkness.

In the fourteenth century, Tibetan Buddhism was enjoying a climate which allowed it to explore the most varied routes, without necessarily renouncing the central path – though temporary

Dâkinî, deity of the bardo.

personal rivalries sometimes tended to discard the principles of tolerance and integrity preached by the Enlightened One. A man of great ability then undertook the restoration of respect for the rules and of preaching by example, revising all the major texts, the *Kanjur* and the *Tanjur*, which he subjected to close scrutiny. "The man from the valley of the onions" was born in 1357 in Amdo, a rugged and backward province which gave Tibet some of its most luminous personalities. Precocious and persevering, Tsongkhapa was initiated in monastic rule from the age of three by the fourth *Karmapa*, chief of the *Karma Kagyü* line.

Of the eighteen works of explication and commentary written by Tsongkhapa which served to train generations of monks, two still enjoy the widespread favor: the *Lam-rim Chenmo*, or "Gradual Path to Enlightenment," and the *Ngagrim Chenmo*, or "Great Explication of the Secret Mantra." His disciples were held to strict observance of monastic rules, particularly celibacy, and Tsongkhapa exercised extreme caution in the transmission of the *tantra*, especially of the esoteric practices.

Je Rimpoche, as the Tibetans devotedly call him, died in his monastery of Ganden in 1419, at the age of sixty-one. Duly embalmed and placed in the *chörten*, his mummified body was the object of unflagging adoration until its destruction during the cultural revolution. Some claim that the Red Guards who assailed it literally became mad with terror on discovering the serene smile of their victim...

CHAPTER 20

MASTER AND DISCIPLE

AN UNSHAKABLE TRUST

ALL SCHOOLS COMBINED, BUDDHISM ABOUNDS WITH ANECDOTES DEMONSTRATING THAT FINDING A MASTER IS NO EASY matter. Already in the time of Çakyamûni, when the Enlightened One was preparing to leave his companions for nirvana and his disciples wept at the loss of their spiritual guide, the Buddha commanded them to be "their own torch." More so even perhaps than in other countries, in Tibet and in the Ch'an and Zen schools, the guru's role is cardinal: it is upon him that rests the duty of leading the pupil by the most appropriate path to the threshold of knowledge, wisdom and Enlightenment.

Nor, similarly, may the candidate for spiritual adventure pick just anyone to guide him on its narrow path. Besides, many famous masters have repeatedly warned against excessive haste in attaching oneself to a guru. This quest and relationship are ideally illustrated by the famous story of Milarêpa and Marpa, the lama with the pitiless requirements who made his pupil pay dearly for youthful misbehavior before granting him the keys that made him not only a famous ascetic, but also a poet whose songs enchant readers and listeners to this very day.

The "man from Mar," as his name indicates,

lived in the eleventh century in southern Tibet. Born into a prominent family, he decided to study Sanskrit with the intention of traveling to India for training at the school of the wise. The sale of his personal property enabled him to undertake the voyage, and, for sixteen years, he followed the instructions of Nâropa, one of the great scholars of the time, a contemporary of Atisha, and also a teacher in Nâlanda. After returning to Tibet, Marpa led a family life, dividing his time between his lay obligations and a remarkable translation activity, interpreting the texts brought back from India. History has preserved a very accurate record of this and the Tibetans call him "Marpa the translator." It was on his return from another trip to India that Mila begged him to accept him as a disciple.

Marpa spared no trial for the aspirant, and only the remonstrances of his wife, Dagmema, dissuaded him from extinguishing the pupil's enthusiasm. While his fame as a translator is not at all diminished, the "man from Mar" also symbolizes the intransigence of the true guru, who, before granting instruction, exacts from his disciple a total gift of himself. In this sense, he is the

Nineteenth-century bronze representing Milarêpa, the poet-ascetic, prototype of the singular relationship between teacher and disciple.

image of the supreme trust that Tibetan Buddhism places in a master seen to be fully enlightened – even though this means sometimes overlooking the fact that he happens to be human.

The Marpa/Milarêpa relationship was also tumultuous because, when he arrived at his master's, the seeker brought with him a weighty past. Having lost his father in infancy, the future ascetic became an expert in black magic to avenge his mother for the humiliations suffered on account of the greed of an uncle. Becoming aware of the villainy of his acts, he then sought forgiveness and applied to Rôngtôn, a renowned Nyingma master, who sent him to Marpa. Approaching the age of forty, Mila placed himself at his service and suffered whims and insults with hardly a murmur until his despair drove him to the edge of suicide. He failed to accomplish this fatal gesture, and, on the strength of this drastic purification of the past, Marpa finally agreed to initiate him into the arcana of supreme knowledge. He taught him the most taxing exercises, including the *tummo*, or inner heat, which Mila practiced for many years in the solitude of the Himalayan caves, particularly at the foot of the sacred mountain of Kaîlash. There he earned the nickname of *rêpa*, "he who wears the cotton robe of the ascetics," and once he had agreed to congregate with men, he attracted many faithful followers. One disciple, Rechungpa set down his exploits and related his life to the great joy of wandering bards and storytellers, who have passed it on from generation to generation.

The example of the perfect yogin who travelled the hard road from the misdeeds of a turbulent youth to the most demanding ordeals, Mila composed *The Hundred Thousand Songs*, one of the brightest jewels of Buddhist literature. He is often represented seated on a gazelle skin posed on a lotus, dressed as a hermit, holding his right hand at his ear, as he listens to the silence. He and his master are considered to be the creators of the Kagyüpa school, founded on the teachings of the *Mahâmûdrâ*, or "Great Seal" and the "Six doctrines of Nâropa," which Marpa brought back from India.

As revealing as the story of this uncommon relationship may be, extraordinary in the personality of its chief protagonists and through the light it sheds on the special bond that is forged between master and disciple, one cannot overlook the equally insightful words of the Buddha. He cautioned that when seeking a relationship with a guru to engage in the quest for knowledge: "You should not believe anything simply because a wise man has said it, because it is generally believed, because it is written, because it is presented as being of the divine essence, or because someone else believes it. Believe only what you yourself judge to be true after you have tested it in the flame of experience."

Preceding double page: gathering in the assembly hall of a Tibetan monastery.
Opposite: young practitioners listening to the teaching.

THE PROTECTOR OF TIBET

CHENRESIG - AVALOKITESHVARA

"HE WHO SEES WITH CLEAR EYES," OR "HE WHO HEARS THE PRAYERS OF THE WORLD," "THE LORD WHO LOOKS DOWN UPON THE Suffering of the World," is a figurehead of the Tibetan tradition. One of the most remarkable Enlightened Beings of the *Mahâyâna*, this Bodhisattva is the patron saint of Tibet, and King Songtsen Gampo was considered to be his incarnation. Like his peers, his essential characteristic is compassion, thus his widespread appellation as the Great Compassionate One, or Lord of Infinite Compassion.

Chenresig is represented in some 108 different forms, described in various texts. Among the thirty commonest, and particularly in Tibet, he is personified with eleven heads and a veritable aureole of arms forming a halo around him: this is Avalokiteshvara (his Sanskrit name) with the thousand arms, each hand adorned with an eye, the better to see the miseries of the world and thus fly instantly to the aid of the needy. His image is always particularly dynamic, although in smaller effigies he is content with four arms, symbolizing all the others he uses to soothe the pains of the world.

According to legend, the Bodhisattva looked at the world one day and was so impressed by what he saw that he temporarily despaired of the scale of the task he had set himself, and his head literally burst with the pain. His spiritual father, the primordial Buddha Amitâbha "of Infinite Light," of whom he is the emanation, gathered the pieces from which he made eleven new heads which Avalokiteshvara wears in three successive series of three faces each. The first reflects compassion, the second wrath with regard to the distress of the world, and the third, the joy engendered by good. The next to last face above these is surmounted by a final head, the head of the Buddha Amitâbha. According to other interpretations, these ten faces refer to the ten steps travelled by the Bodhisattva until he attains Buddhahood.

Chenresig is especially dear to Tibetans because he is believed to have started the historic Yarlung dynasty whose founder, Nyatri Sangpo, grandfather of Songtsen Gampo, is believed to be his incarnation. In the classical canon of representation of this figure, six of the eight arms attached to his shoulders each bear a specific symbol: rosary, lotus, Wheel of the Law, jar of nectar, while the last two form the *anjâli mûdrâ*. The

The many faces of the tutelary divinity of the Land of the Snows.

remaining 992 arms all have the eye of mercy in the open palm, open to the suffering to be soothed. His sacred mantra is *om mani peme hung*, probably the first to have made its appearance in Tibet, and, for practicing Buddhists, still the most popular.

Very often shown upright on the traditional lotus throne, like most Tibetan deities, whether peaceful or wrathful, Chenresig often holds a lotus flower in one of his hands: hence his occasional appellation of Padmapâni (Lotus Bearer). Moreover, Avalokiteshvara is directly associated with certain lines of wisdom throughout the Buddhist world, where he assumes rather striking local traits in the different latitudes. Thus, in China and Japan, the Bodhisattva of Compassion has been feminized and is the object of popular worship under the features of Kuan-Yin and Kwannon respectively.

Because of his thousand arms, Chenresig is also credited with a singular power of influence in favoring good and in lessening the sufferings of the beings of the six realms of existence. In various forms, he dispenses comfort and aid, both to animals and to famished spirits, and naturally to human beings. These last are in fact privileged, in so far as, possessing self-consciousness, they alone enjoy the incomparable fortune of being able to open their eyes to their condition of being, and even decide to take the path of Enlightenment which leads to the shedding of illusion. Besides, and by no means the least of his salient features, in Tibetan eyes the Dalai Lama is an incarnation of Avalokiteshvara, of the All Compassionate, and, as such, the veneration surrounding him is directed at once towards himself and towards the illustrious deity of whom he is the living representative in the world of men.

Nineteenth-century bronze representing Chenresig-Avalokiteshvara with eleven heads and four pairs of arms.

CHAPTER 22

TÂRÂ DRÖLMA

GUARDIAN, PROTECTRESS AND SAVIOR

CLOSELY ASSOCIATED WITH CHENRESIG, TÂRÂ DRÖLMA IS VIRTUALLY INSEPARABLE FROM THE BODHISATTVA OF COMPASSION. She personifies the feminine aspect of his solicitude and actively assists him. Considered as the force, power or energy of the deity, dynamism is her essence. It is thus not surprising to find her represented in twenty-one different forms, varying in color, posture and attribution, although she remains first and foremost the "Savior."

Various legends, always closely linked to Chenresig, are attached to her birth. Some say that Târâ Drölma was born of a tear shed by Avalokiteshvara, momentarily dismayed at the vast scale of his mission, others that she was engendered by a blue ray emanating from the eye of the deity, and others still that, from a tear of Chenresig, sprang a lotus, on which Târâ instantly appeared. It is in Tibet that she has the largest number of followers, having been popularized by the devotion paid her by Atisha in particular, being his tutelary divinity. Her popularity persists with many believers who continue to invoke her in one or another of her many aspects.

Two of the many Târâs are of particular importance: the white and the green. Since it is not clearly known which has precedence, they are generally considered as equals. Both are clothed like Bodhisattva and richly ornamented, installed on lotus thrones, holding a lotus flower in the hand – in full bloom for the white and blue – half-open for the green. Moreover, so highly do the Tibetans esteem Târâ, that they made the two beautiful foreign princesses who married King Songtsen Gampo incarnations of the goddess – white for the Chinese Wencheng, green for the Nepalese Bhrikuti Devi. Both are benevolent aspects of the deity.

When endowed with a precise color, the Târâs are directly related to the five original Buddhas as the active power of the Tantric deities. Thus, in Tibet, the blue Târâ bears the name of Ekjatâ and was subjugated by the sage Padmasambhava, who made her an acolyte of the green Târâ. In this case she holds a cleaver and skull in the hand, and presents a ferocious aspect of the goddess. The yellow Târâ, "the Goddess of the Frowning Brows," born of a frown on the face of Avalokiteshvara, is another wrathful form of green Târâ, whose characteristic attributes she carries in her arms (*vajra*, rope, bow, conch shell). Representing the power of love of the original

Consort of Chenresig, Târâ symbolizes the active energy of the deity and appears in twenty-one different aspects.

Târâ, Kurukullâ the red has a gentle appearance, but the bow with which she is armed and her crown of skulls attest to the vigor of her acts.

The white Târâ, also sometimes called Sitatârâ, in bronze or any other uncolored sculpture material, is distinguished by her seven eyes: one normal pair, an eye in each hand, one on the sole of each foot, and one on the forehead. Whether depicted in paintings, on wall frescoes or embroidered on cloth (thangka), her many eyes are always carefully delineated. She is considered to be the country's supreme protector, both guardian of its Buddhist traditions and savior of the faithful, who never hesitate to call on her for help in even minor daily tribulations. Gifted with a variety of powers, Târâ is the guardian of all fear. She appears as soon as a follower calls. She arrives, ready to put to right the most terrible of situations. She protects the faithful from the threat of lions, of elephants, of poisonous snakes or brigands. She also opens the door to impenetrable dungeons and loosens the chains that shackle prisoners. Healer of leprosy, she keeps the fear of death at bay, helps to overcome pain, and to lead pupils to the perfection of supreme accomplishment. She is attributed with unequalled power when faced with lightning, the fury of the oceans, or fire.

According to the *Tantra of Târâ*, during the era of the Victorious, known as the "Light of the many worlds," through her meritous actions and her fervor, the princess Moon of Wisdom was encouraged to pray in order that she should be reborn a man in which state she might reach full Enlightenment. She replied: "In this life no distinction is made between 'masculine' and 'feminine', any more than is made between 'oneself' and 'others', to the extent that even to attach oneself to the idea is senseless. Beings of weak heart allow themselves to be trapped by this illusion. And as there are numerous people who wish to attain Enlightenment in masculine form, for my part I wish to proceed in a feminine body to the benefit of all being until the end of the *samsâra*." It was following this wish that the princess became the goddess Târâ.

It goes without saying that, like all the other emblematic expressions, the symbolic interpretations of Târâ and of her twenty-one aspects are intensified as the seeker advances on the path of knowledge. The close links between Chenresig-Avalokiteshvara and Târâ Drölma naturally make the latter one of the most powerful protectors of the different lines of wisdom, particularly of the Dalai Lamas.

Preceding double page: details of a thangka, the white Târâ, recognizable by her seven "thankful eyes." Opposite: green Târâ, a principal aspect of the Great Protector.

CHAPTER 23

THE GREAT PROTECTORS

MASTERS OF TIME, DEATH AND NEGATIVE FORCES

THESE ARE THE FIERCE GUARDIANS OF THE LAW AND FAITHFUL DEFENDERS OF THE BUDDHA. OFTEN THEY ARE PRE-BUDDHIST deities, unmitigating in their opposition to the messengers of compassion from beyond the Himalayas. Sages and mages strove vigorously to tame them, finally inducing them into service of the doctrine. They thus exemplify the metamorphosis of the disciple transmuting aggressiveness and violence into forces for good. By an unfortunate misunderstanding, essentially due to fragmentary knowledge and hasty interpretations, the so-called ferocious deities have given the Tibetans a bad reputation as devil worshipers. Yet their spiritual masters had simply devised an original manner to signify the complementary polarities, positive and negative, gentle and wrathful, rooted in the human mind.

One of these is Mahâkâla, the "Great Black One," the lord of time and Transcendent Wisdom, whose physical appearance is revealing: with a powerful black warrior's body, protruding teeth and bulging eyes, he bears the sword, a skull cup, and a conch shell or victory banner as he rides the snow tiger or lion, unless he is treading on a pig, snake or cock, emblematic of the three poisons. He symbolizes the strength that destroys the illusion which hinders the attainment of Enlightenment. He is the other face of Chenresig.

Other equally ambivalent ferocious deities include Yamântaka, the slayer of the lord of death, and Pälden Lhamo, the only feminine expression among the great ferocious protective deities. She forms a couple with Mahâkâla, and her origin dates back to the Hindu goddess Shrî Devî. Carried on a red mule, her hair bristling ferociously around her head, she wears a necklace of skulls and her distinctive attribute is an umbrella of peacock feathers. A bloodstained head of an enemy of her religion often hangs from her saddle. In painting and embroidery, she often has an aureole of flames expressing her dynamic activity. A third eye normally adorns her forehead, and the grin she wears revealing two protruding teeth is far from reassuring. She has nevertheless been dubbed "the Glorious Goddess," often has a moon in her hair and a sun on her navel, and is considered as the guardian of Lhasa.

These three ferocious and powerful personages are the official protectors of the order of the Gelugpa, and their tutelary power makes them the privileged guardians of the Dalai Lama.

Nineteenth-century mask of Mahâkâla, the "Great Black One" of Transcendent Wisdom.

CHAPTER 24

THE FIRE RITUAL

THE GREAT PURIFICATION

AS IN MOST CIVILIZATIONS, FROM EARLIEST TIMES UNTIL NOW, FIRE OCCUPIES A SPECIAL PLACE IN BUDDHISM. A FUNDAMENTAL emblematic element, an unavoidable step on the path of knowledge, an integral part of offering because it is both heat and light, fire symbolizes, above all, purification and the flame of impermanence in development and change. In a country where wood is somewhat scarce, the funeral pyre was generally reserved for great accomplished masters, only the most revered being embalmed. The Buddha himself was cremated, and though his physical body left no ash, some bone fragments were recovered by the faithful and set in eight great stupa. Sometimes, as trace of their passage, the great mystics leave behind multi-colored beads, called *ringsel*, testifying to their spiritual accomplishments. Their followers regard these as precious talismans.

Today, still, as in previous times, fire remains the most powerful purifier. In the case of sickness, sometimes to liberate a place or being from a harmful influence, or to assure that a location is propitious for building, a lama is summoned to perform the fire ritual, which is thoroughly codified and must be meticulously executed. If not, the perverse force may inadvertently prevail and

wreak havoc which can only be overcome by a superior power. This also explains why, before starting the ceremony, its officiant must himself submit to prior exercises of perfect purification.

Juniper, incense, and all sorts of other aromatic woods can be burned. Depending on the extent of the evil to be countered or overcome, one or more monks are asked to exert their combined talents, generally accompanied by the recitation of mantra or *dhârani*, the making of specific gestures (*mûdrâ*) and the playing of the ritual tambourine (*damaru*) to enhance the effectiveness of the overall performance.

It is worth noting, although it should come as no surprise, that certain striking correspondences exist between the Tibetan fire ritual and ceremonies aimed at similar purposes in the Hopi Amerindian tradition. This shared practice forms a bridge across the Pacific, beyond time and human memory, standing as the reminder of a deep spiritual brotherhood which, over the ages, has come to be forgotten.

Opposite: the essence of purification.
Following double page: incense during a ritual fire ceremony.

CHAPTER 25

MONKS AND LAITY

A DENSELY WOVEN SOCIAL FABRIC

UNTIL THE CHINESE INVASION IN 1950, TIBET WAS UNDOUBTEDLY A WORLD APART ON A PLANET WHERE SOCIAL UPHEAVAL WAS causing sweeping changes. A still feudal society impregnated with theocracy, apart from and above all others, the Land of the Snows preserved the structures of another age. Yet the few eyewitnesses who went there all reported a primitive society, though one not lacking in refinement, and, above all, a harmonious social structure, with a population that was frugal but smiling and content with life.

Reflecting this equilibrium, monks and laity lived in symbiosis. Monks depended on the latter for food and accommodation, since it was the laity who cultivated the land and brought in the harvests. In return, monks were expected to guarantee the spiritual well-being of all. Tradition expected one child of each family to become a monk, which was considered an honor. The noviciate generally began at the age of eight, while monastic vows could only be taken after twenty.

As a rule, the entire lay population observed five basic precepts common to all Buddhists (not to kill, not to steal, and to avoid verbal and sexual

misconduct, as well as the use of intoxicating substances). The obligations of novices were more restrictive: to abstain from destroying any living creature, from claiming what is not given, from erotic conduct, from liquor and drugs that lead to carelessness, from eating at undue times, from dancing, singing and going to shows, from wearing garlands and perfume, from sitting or sleeping on a couch or in luxury, and from accepting money. Lay persons could receive a so-called daily ordination from time to time in the eight precepts of the *Mâhayâna*, or the basic vows of the novices, provided they retake them whenever they wished to put them into practice.

Tibetan monks, like all *bhikshu* of all the Buddhist schools, are required to practice the strict monastic discipline codified in the *Vinaya* set down in the time of the Buddha. The simple ordination ceremony which marks the entry into the *sangha*, is synonymous with deep commitment and is the occasion for festivities. It should be remembered that the monastic tradition was originally to wander like the historical Buddha after Enlightenment, spreading and explaining the doctrine, and that communal life was limited to the three months of the rainy season.

Eighteenth-century bronze of a monk teaching.

CHAPTER 26

THE MEDITATOR

MEMORY OF THE CENTURIES

THE HERMIT AND ASCETIC, OFTEN WANDER-
ERS, HAVE BEEN AN ESSENTIAL COMPONENT
OF ASIA'S RELIGIOUS TRADITION SINCE TIME
immemorial. Tibetan Buddhism is no exception,
and the vastness of the Land of the Snows is particularly propitious to solitary reflection so dear to
the great masters. It was, in fact, formerly the custom to prepare huts and caves lying outside the
monastic enclosure to enable aspirants to practice
retreats of varying length under the guidance of a
guru, relying on the generosity of the community
for a minimum of subsistence.

The classic retreat, common to all orders,
traditionally lasts three years and three months
in solitary, and can be repeated often during a
lifetime. It cannot, however, be done without the
consent or enlightened guidance of a master,
who in some way shares the responsibility with
the disciple in training. This was current in all
the great monasteries of Tibet, and is perpetuated
today in Tibetan Buddhist study centers that
have sprung up throughout the world in the
Buddhist diaspora. Some believe that this rigorous training tradition originated in the annual
retreat made by the members of the *sangha* in the
time of the Buddha during the three months of
the rainy season. This tradition is still practiced

in the Buddhist countries of Southeast Asia.

Nevertheless, while the full-time meditator
may be in retreat from the world, he is not totally
withdrawn from it – with a few rare exceptions.
By training himself in this way, he prepares to put
the knowledge he thus acquires at the service of
others and of society when he returns among
men. Inured to the ordeal of a rigorous discipline,
he (or she) is presumed to have surmounted most
of the obstacles (particularly the three poisons of
ignorance, hatred and desire) of daily life, thus
enabling him to play a beneficial role for all.

In everyday life, he who meditates regularly
without necessarily renouncing his routine obligations, seeks primarily to harmonize his interior
life with the existence he leads. Yet, among all
practitioners, on their own scale, it is their full
and conscious participation in a multi-secular
chain of uninterrupted transmission of an essential wisdom, which, in its most accomplished
expressions, permits full detachment in the midst
of universal bonds.

The classic position in meditation,
designed to gather and channel one's energies.

CHAPTER 27

PILGRIMAGE

SIGN-POSTS IN THE TERRITORY OF THE SACRED

ALL RELIGIONS, FROM THE RUDIMENTARY TO THE MOST EXPANSIVE, HAVE IN COMMON SPECIFIC PLACES OF REFERENCE WHICH ASSUME particular importance for their followers. In their eyes, this singular aura marks out a territory traveled mentally as often as desired, and physically as many times as possible, but, depending on the follower's means, at least once in a lifetime. A parenthesis if not a break, a journey of pilgrimage, however long, provides an opportunity to leave daily contingencies behind in order to evaluate one's quest so far and devote oneself to reflection.

An inherently nomadic people, Tibetans are no exception. Born walkers, they are quick to break with the daily grind and depart on the trails of holy vagrancy, whether alone, in families or even by whole villages or clans. Naturally, like all Buddhists of any school, the places directly associated with the life of the Enlightened One hold a special place in their hearts. Quite often, however, these places scattered within the confines of what was formerly the Kingdom of Magadha (approximately the Bihar of today's India) have been virtually inaccessible. Only wandering ascetics and the most demanding seekers of the absolute took the time to undertake this hazardous voyage from which they knew they might never return.

Bodh Gaya has been frequented for more than two millennia by adepts from all over the Buddhist world, come to bow at the foot of the *pipal* tree where the historical Buddha crossed the threshold of full Enlightenment. Today, a sleepy little village, often crushed by the heat, it keeps alive the memory of the exceptional moment, and hums with the serene activities of monks from all schools permanently established in its monasteries where study and prayer suffice to fill many a lifetime. Sometimes, on the occasion of a special event or particular initiation, the holy city swells with an unaccustomed human presence and becomes, for a few hours or days, a spiritual center vibrating with energy – an unforgettable event for those that experience it.

Sarnath, not far from the immemorial holy city of Varanasi, testifies, by the venerable stupa of the Emperor Ashoka, to the first teaching of the Enlightened One, the deer of its park recalling his first adepts. An enduring gentleness pervades this place where, upon the ruined foundations of ancient monasteries, others have sprung up to safeguard a heritage which, despite all vicissitudes, has withstood the ravages of time.

Mount Kailash in western Tibet is one of the most popular places of pilgrimage in the Buddhist and Hindu world.

In Lumbini, today in the Nepalese lowlands, near Kapilavastu, the capital of the Shakya Kingdom of which nothing now remains, clear evidence has been found which indicates that this was Prince Siddharta's actual birthplace: Ashoka had a stupa erected there with tablets containing detailed information. Their authenticity has been corroborated by a year of intensive study since they came to light in 1995. And in Kushinagara, formerly a small village totally undistinguished from thousands of others, the Buddha stretched out on his side and, before entering *nirvana*, bestowed a final command to his tearful disciples: "Be a light unto yourselves."

So much for historical sites. The others, and there are many, dot the vast territory where the Buddhist light passed and was sometimes momentarily extinguished. In India itself, Sanchi boasted a magnificent stupa, while the Caves of Ajanta and Ellora bear witness to the sacred through beauty, and Borobodur in Java attests to the faith of its inspired builders by a unique stone mandala. The colossal statues of Gal Vihara near Polonaruwa in Sri Lanka are stunning in their timeless harmony, and ancient Siam, Burma, Afghanistan, Japan, Korea, China and Mongolia have all, each in their own way, contributed their jewels to the edification of Buddhist art, transforming selected places into inexhaustible sources of replenishment. Nor did Tibet lag behind.

Since Buddhism has metamorphosed the deities of earlier religions into expressions of the Good Law, it is hardly surprising to find sacred lakes and mountains, the reward of a breathtaking natural beauty, upon the solitary vastness. Thus Amnye Machen in the east responds to the even more royal grandeur of Kailash, the mythical Mount Meru and axis of the world of Indian tradition, which became Kang Rimpoche (Precious Venerable of Snowy Peaks) for the faithful. This is one of Tibet's great places of pilgrimage, undoubtedly one of the most difficult of access with the passage of the Dölma Pass at an altitude of 21,882 feet, though also one of the most impressive. The Himalayan panorama unfolds in serene splendor, inducing in the traveler a physical awareness of his natural links with a world impregnated with the seal of an ineradicable and ubiquitous spirituality.

A place may become sacred even though fashioned by the labor of men. One such site is Lhasa, the capital of Tibet, which means "holy place." The Potala, the imposing red and white palace that towers above the city – until only recently the winter residence of the Dalai Lamas and the seat of government – bears the name of the celestial dwelling of Avalokiteshvara, the tutelary divinity of the Land of the Snows, whose ever-present incarnation on earth is the Dalai Lama . . . Nesting symbols that interlock with each other, mutiple and myriad facets of a living legend of infinite duration, and footholds of a particular geography of the sacred.

Monks on a pilgrimage.

CHAPTER 28

THE PASSAGE OF DEATH

THERE IS NEITHER BEGINNING NOR END

INTEGRATING DEATH WITH LIFE IS AN EVERY-DAY FACT FOR THE TIBETANS, OR AT LEAST FOR MANY OF THEM. ONE CANNOT EXIST without the other, and the cardinal notion of impermanence or rebirth reveals therein the touchstone of a way of life. "Sooner or later," says the Dalai Lama, "death will come. To think about it and prepare for it may prove useful when it arrives. If you believe only in this life, and disagree that life continues, being aware or unaware of death is irrelevant. If another life exists, however, it may be useful to be ready for death, because in this way one is less terrified of its process, and the situation is not complicated by one's own thoughts." For the Tibetan sage, meditation on death is equivalent to the exploration of a territory with uncertain landmarks.

In Tibetan tradition, the Lord of Death is a ferocious deity of wrathful mien. He is Yamantaka, "the Destroyer of the Lord of Death," a meditation deity peculiar to the Gelugpa school. He is the other face of Mañjushrî, the Bodhisattva of Peerless Insightful Wisdom, whose attributes are the volume of Perfection of Wisdom texts and the sword that cleaves the bonds of ignorance.

Eighteenth-century bronze, one of the
six deities who accompany the deceased to the bardo.

Yamantaka is represented with several heads, the central one of which is that of a bull, and many pairs of arms and feet, dancing in union with his consort, Vajravetalî, upon a host of human, animal and demonic forms. This ambivalence expresses the Buddhist conception of perpetual metamorphosis which governs existence itself. The deeply anchored feeling that death is part of the natural order of things does not preclude its consideration by rites. On the contrary, the moribund is accompanied that he or she might take the steps of this end of the road with serenity, and when the life principle has departed the body, prayers and ceremonies continue to convey him safely home upon the twisted trails of the limbo of the *bardo*. The officiating lama or an astrologer is consulted to determine the ordering of the rites and the most propitious moment for their performance.

For Tibetans, the world beyond life is peopled by unusual creatures, who are actually simply projections of the human mind, and whose symbolism merely reflects its fears and anxieties. Thus the *citipati*, or pyre masters, are acolytes of Yama and are commonly represented in pairs or couples of dancing skeletons in the company of ferocious deities. In the eyes of the faithful, they illustrate the ephemeral nature of existence and are emblematic of the cessation of earthly attachments and suffering.

Feminine energies are personified by the dâkinî (khandroma) and, whether benevolent or wrathful, these always play an active role with the masculine deities. They guide the seeker in his quest, as well as the intermediary being in his passage through the bardo. Often represented by fine and well-proportioned female figures, but with slightly menacing facial expressions, only their attributes – kapâla, skull necklace and sword – declare their nature, provoking the faithful to turn them into allies rather than adversaries.

Once abandoned by the breath of life, whose best point of exit is the apex of the skull, the corpse must be returned to one of its component elements: fire, water, earth, air. Victims of infectious diseases, leprosy or smallpox, are normally buried. Inhumation is reserved for the great ones of this world (king to tomb, sage to chörten) after being embalmed and dressed in precious apparel. Some perfectly accomplished sages are thought to have the gift of literally "dissolving" at the ideal moment, into what is called "a rainbow body."

The lack of sufficient wood makes cremation an exceptional event. The custom of "celestial funerals" (ja-gor) is the most widespread and is practiced in a place often reserved near a monastery by the members of the Ragyapa corporation. They take charge of ritually dismembering the corpses in the presence of an officiating lama and a handful of relatives and friends of the deceased, and the pieces are then thrown to birds of prey. For the Tibetans, this is action stands as the ultimate testimony of their non-attachment to a transient body, and of solidarity with other creatures who feed on its remains.

Just as in the Middle Ages, Europe had its "Arts of Dying," since Buddhists do not have the slightest doubt about reincarnation, the Tibetans too have a guide to avoid the pitfalls on the narrow path leading from one life to another. This is the famous Bardo Thôdol, or "Tibetan Book of the Dead," of which the first western translation at the turn of the century made a sensation. The book is read by the officiating priest into the ear of the dying person, explaining to him the steps of his travels and enjoining on him to avoid succumbing to fear while crossing unknown realms, to undo bonds without returning to frighten the living, and to seize the opportunity presented and apprehend the luminous clarity when he encounters it. It is specifically for the success of this delicate passage that practitioners strive in meditation to chart a map of this territory strewn with pitfalls, in order to experience their death in full awareness, the indispensable prerequisite for good rebirth – unless they acknowledge the profound and real significance of the Great Light, thereby definitively breaking the circle of reincarnations. The person thus freed from the chains of ignorance attains Enlightenment.

The citipati, acolytes of the Lord of Death.

CHAPTER 29

THE DALAI LAMA

INCARNATION OF THE DIVINE

OCEAN OF WISDOM, INCOMPARABLE MAS-
TER, YISHIN NORBU OR WISH-FULFILLING
JEWEL, PRECIOUS VICTORIOUS OR GYALWA
Rimpoche, Lord of the White Lotus, or simply
Kundün, the Presence: so many titles among a
host of others express at once the power, knowledge, benevolence and compassion the Tibetans
use to evoke the most illustrious and the most
revered among their number, the Dalai Lama.

An exceptional being, perennially surround-
ed by legend and mystery, the fourteenth of the
line today, acknowledged but exiled Holder of the
Lion's Throne, Tenzin Gyatso has shouldered the
heavy burden for his people of being their spiritual
guide in a period of impenetrable darkness, and
their temporal leader at a turning point in history
marked both by rthe cruel ordeal of foreign occupation and the necessity of opening up the country
to the outside and to modernity. If he is today a
thoroughly familiar symbol of Tibetan Buddhism
throughout the world, it is this monk with his
piercing gaze and infectious smile who represents
his living faith as sell as Tibet itself, the survival
of which hangs in the balance. Whatever tran-
spires, the Tibetans of the diaspora and of the
interior continue to recognize in him their sole
spiritual and temporal authority.

The historic institution of the Dalai Lama is
rooted in Buddhism's fundamental concept of
reincarnation: every being, whoever he may be,
bears in himself the seed of Enlightenment, and
will ultimately achieve it, even if his path is prolonged in time. Hence the inescapable necessity
of the circle of births for its attainment. Yet some
are more skillful than others, and, by working
assiduously on themselves, they get there faster.
In the course of successive lives, they choose and
they affirm, thereby becoming capable of select-
ing the form in which they will return to complete this development. This is the privilege of a
chosen few whom the Tibetans call *tulku* (literally, "bodies of transformation"), reincarnations of
masters, who return in a renewed body to complete the task they have undertaken.

This tradition was consolidated in Tibet in
the thirteenth century with the discovery of the
second Karmapa, leader of the Kagyü school, and
was subsequently confirmed for other great masters, thus guaranteeing the permanent transmission of knowledge from generation to generation, but also a much questioned political

*Tenzin Gyatso, fourteenth of the line of
teachers of wisdom, the present holder of the Lion's Throne,
spiritual and temporal leader (in exile) of Tibetans and of Tibet.*

continuity. The actual line of the Dalai Lamas is a late phenomenon (dating from the sixteenth century) set up in the wake of the establishment of the Gelugpa order founded by the reformer Tsongkhapa. Yet the title itself, which means "Master of Wisdom Greater than the Ocean" (or Ocean of Wisdom), comes from *tale lama*, attributed by the Mongol Prince Altan Khan to his spiritual master Sonam Gyatso, at that time head of the school of the Yellow Hats. He retrospectively granted it to his two predecessors, of whom the first, Gendün Drup (1391- 475) was one of the closest disciples of Tsongkhapa.

It is with the Great Fifth Lobsang Gyatso (1617-1682) that spiritual and temporal powers became inextricably merged for greater effectiveness on the Tibetan national scene until the Chinese invasion of 1949/1950. The tradition of the *tulku* has survived in exile, despite obstacles posed by the difficult conditions of the moment, as testified by the dispute which broke out in 1995 between the Dalai Lama and the Chinese Government in Beijing concerning the reincarnation of the Pänchen Lama, the second religious hierarch of Tibetan Buddhism, whose fate is closely linked to that of the Dalai Lama and hence to the very future of Tibet.

There is no doubt that, to Tibetan eyes, the Dalai Lama is a being completely apart. Tradition, his education, his charisma, his power, his erudition, and the veneration he enjoys, certainly make him an outstanding person, but there is something besides: a subtle alchemy of uninterrupted exchange between his people and himself. For them, not only is he the protector, incarnation of the Bodhisattva of Infinite Compassion himself, but also the personification of a lost land and the token of its permanence, the promise of return.

It must be admitted that the life of Tenzin Gyatso, recognized fourteenth Dalai Lama at the tender age of two and a half on a modest farm in a village in Amdo (eastern Tibet, today incorporated in the Chinese province of Qinghai), has been far from ordinary. "Simple Buddhist monk" as he calls himself, he is nonetheless a key personality of contemporary history, whose role on the international scene was acknowledged by the bestowal of the Nobel Peace Prize in 1989.

Born in the village of Takster, on – according to the lunar calendar – the fifth day of the fifth month of the year of the wood pig (6 July 1935), the fourteenth Dalai Lama was recognized by a mission of high religious dignitaries, and subsequently conveyed, in October 1938, to Lhasa where he was enthroned on the Lion Throne on 22 February 1940. For the lively spirited and turbulent boy this marked the start of a rigorous and virtually solitary training under the vigilant gaze of his two tutors, both outstanding scholars. Yet beyond the formidable Himalayan ramparts, events followed one another in quick succession, the Second World War brought the world into conflict, empires vanished and countries emerged, and China was torn asunder between nationalists and communists. Mao and his troops finally prevailed and the new power established in Beijing in 1949 immediately announced its intention to "liberate Tibet." This was quickly materialized in military invasion and occupation, a stranglehold that persists to this day, marked in 1959 by a popular anti-Chinese revolt that was quelled in bloodshed. This date also marked the exile of the Dalai Lama and some hundred thousand Tibetans, mostly refugees to India, but also scattered throughout every other continent.

For Tenzin Gyatso, these years of ordeal opened up the world, but he has never lost sight of what he considers his essential mission for his people and his country in these difficult times: to save Tibet and its great civilization, to safeguard its spiritual wealth and unique heritage. Having, so to speak, renewed the secular tradition of the wandering monk, the Dalai Lama is undoubtedly no ordinary pilgrim. He is fully aware that his path is still strewn with many boulders, but the attention he awakens in his audience, the deference he enjoys, and the answers he offers to questions facing our world, encourage him to persevere in the hope of returning home and in a spirit of determined nonviolence.

Questioned about his own future, the Dalai Lama ceaselessly repeats that, like the Buddha himself, he is merely a man, and that his compassion and his profound understanding go to his fellows, all other human beings, and to their suffering. "We're just visiting," he says, "tourists making experiments, just passing through. Without tolerance or dialogue, we make our own lives unbearable, and, besides, we harm our environment. All we need is a small effort to make our world more livable for everyone, free from the violence that erodes and destroys everything."

And he continues: "Tibet is perfectly viable without a Dalai Lama. It thrived for centuries before the institution existed as such, and, theoretically, it's perfectly conceivable. Human institutions pass, and whether they continue or not is a matter of circumstances. In absolute terms, Tibet, its nation, its culture, and even Buddhism, are perfectly conceivable without a Dalai Lama. For the time being, the Dalai Lama is a symbol, a symbol of Tibet. This is why he is important. Later on, in thirty or forty years, who knows? Everything changes. Incidentally, there will always be human beings who possess the requisite qualities to be a Dalai Lama. The incarnations of Buddhas or Bodhisattvas continue to be manifested whatever happens . . . And not only in human form."

Following double page: the Potala, the winter palace of the Dalai Lama and formerly the seat of the Tibetan government in Lhasa.

CHAPTER 30

THE LOTUS

DARKNESS AND LIGHT

THE LOTUS FLOWER, WHICH IS OMNIPRESENT IN BUDDHIST REPRESENTATIONS, SEEMS INDISSOCIABLE FROM THE DEITIES WHO POPULATE this world where, closely intermingled, shadow and light relentlessly play hide-and-seek on the Eightfold Path to Enlightenment. The lotus has been a cardinal symbol from the beginning of Indian Vedic times, when the palette of its colors and the phases of its flowering were skillfully used to transmit precise meanings: blossoming or in bud, white, pink, red or blue, it is associated with definite aspects of teaching, or of wisdom, of which it expresses a given revealing feature.

An implicit reminder of the true nature of man, the lotus refers to him by analogy: born in the mire of stagnant ponds, once it has traversed the perfidious sweetness of the water, like a miracle of harmony perpetually renewed, it emerges and blossoms in the air or on the surface. The fascination it has exerted on the human mind for so long led the artists of Asia to use it as the privileged seat for all Buddhas and Bodhisattva, while at the same time it is one of the most regular attributes of the protective and compassionate deities. Chenresig, the official Protector of the Land of the Snows, is incarnate among men in his emanation, the Dalai Lama, who bears the title of Lord of the White Lotus, a color which by itself embodies all others and symbolizes the spiritual perfection of the Buddha.

The pink lotus is the prerogative of Siddharta, the historical Buddha. The red lotus signifies compassion, or the original nature of the Bodhisattva, and is then directly associated with Avalokiteshvara-Chenresig. The blue lotus, always shown in bud, is a distinctive emblem of Manjushri, Bodhisattva of wisdom, he who is the image of the victory of mind over matter.

Its dual nature also makes the lotus a solar symbol, in so far as the variations of its blossoms are declinated in direct accordance with the power of the sun. Its eight stylized petals naturally refer to the Eightfold Path, and it accompanies the Tibetans in their solitary intonations. It may symbolize the Buddha himself, and even his dual aspect, masculine and feminine. Between the corolla and the stem, there is also a complementarity, expressed in the interrelationship between shadow and light that sculpts the highs and lows of daily existence.

Lotus: the sacred flower of Buddhism.

GLOSSARY

BARDO: intermediary state, between death and subsequent rebirth

BHIKSHU/BHIKSHUNI: monk, nun

BODHISATTVA: enlightened person whose compassion impels him to renounce nirvana for the sake of all suffering beings

BÖNPO: pre-Buddhist religious ideas in Tibet

CHAKRA/KHORLO: wheel, disc, circle, symbol of Buddist teaching

CHAM: ceremonial religious dances

CHATURMAHARÂJÂ: counting markers of the Tibetan rosary

CHÖRTEN/STUPA: Buddhist sanctuary, tower to hold relics, funerary monument or mound

CINTAMANI: magic gem that satisfies all desires, symbol of the free spirit

DAKÎNÎ: female deity

DAMARU: small ritual drum

DHARMA: Buddhist law

DOB-DOB: monk or guardian of order in monasteries

DORJE/VAJRA: thunderbolt

DRILBU/GHANTA: ritual bell

GARUDA: mythical bird

GELUGPA: Buddhist school founded in the 14th century by the reformer Tsongkhapa to which the Dalai Lama belongs

GRIGUG/KARTÎKA: ritual chopper

GYALING: musical instrument

KADAMPA: school of Tibetan Buddhism

KAGYUPA: school of oral transmission, founded by Marpa, and of which

the poet-ascetic Milarêpa is one of the best known representatives

KÂLACHAKRA: Wheel of Time, the highest level of Buddhism initiation

KALASHA: vase, cup (generally holding the Elixir of Life)

KANGLING: musical instrument

KAPÂLA: skull cup or bowl

KARMA: law of causalty in Buddhist philosophy

KARMAPA: head of the Tibetan Buddhist School of Kagyupa

KHATA: the Kagyupa ceremonial scarf, scarf of happiness

KHORTEN: prayer wheel

LAM-RIM CHENMO: major work of Tsongkapa, "The Gradual Path to Enlightenment"

LUNGTA: wind-horse, good luck charm

MADHYAMÎKA: philosophical schools of the Middle Way

MAHASIDDHA: "Great Adept," 84 saints and sages of the Vajrayâna

MAHÂYÂNA: school of the Great Vehicle

MÂLA: rosary of 108 beads

MANDALA: mystic circle, perfected geometrically-divided environment of the divine universe or residence

MANI: abbreviation of the sacred formula "om mani peme hum"

MANTRA: mystic invocation

MÖNLAM CHENMO: great prayer for the happiness of all beings

MÛDRÂ: ritual sacred gesture

NIRVANA: state of perfect and eternal happiness, paradise

NORBU: precious jewel

NYINGMAPA: oldest order of Tibetan Buddhism, founded in the 18th century by Padmasambhava

PADMA/PEMA: lotus flower

PARINIRVANA: final nirvana, death of the historical Buddha

PHURBU: ritual dagger

RADONG: musical horn

SADHANA: ritual of description and devotion or formula for the invocation of a god

SANGHA: monastic community

SAPTARATNA/RINCHEN NA-DUN: the seven precious treasures

STUPA: see chorten

TANTRA: mystic ritual, basis of esoteric Tantrism

THANGKA: scroll painting on silk or cotton

THERAVADA: school of the small vehicule

TORMA: offering of flour and butter

TSAMPA: barley flour, staple of Tibetan food

TSOK: offering

TÜLKU: reincarnated body

VAJRA/DORJE: thunderbolt

VAJRAYÂNA/TANTRAYÂNA: school of the Diamond Way, particular to Tibet

VINAYA: Buddhist code of discipline

YIDAM: archeype, archetypal deity, personal guardian of the faithful, principal deity of the mandala

ACKNOWLEDGMENTS

To all those who, through their knowledge and expertise, have contributed to this book in an atmosphere of cordial collaboration. To Marc-Alain Ouaknin, for his helpful hints. To Alessandri, fantastic realist painter, who generously put his collection at Giaveno at our disposal. To Claudio Tecchio at Carmagnola, and Bruno Portigliatti at Giaveno. To Mema d'Evionnaz, Sushil Lama, Pasang, and all the team at the Happy Valley Guesthouse, Katmandu. To Tenzin Geyche Tethong and the venerable Lhakdor, at Péma-la, Dharamsala. To my first and most faithful, ever-present reader. To His Holiness the Dalai Lama who showed me the Path.

The Editor would like to thank Jean-Claude Buhrer-Solal for his contribution to the photographs; Sumand Shyamananad, advisory minister at the Royal Embassy of Nepal; and all the monasteries in Bodnath for their warm welcome. Also, Philippe Sebirot for his assistance in creating the photographs, along with Daniel Delisle, Frédéric Lenoir, Jacqueline Hartley and Adeline for their help in making this book.

PHOTO CREDITS:
J.-Cl. Buhrer-Solal p.13, 19, 11, 122-123 and 129. Planet © Olivier Föllmi p.17 and 27.

WORKS CITED:
Dalai Lama quotations, pages 38 and 60, taken from Awakening the Mind, Lightening the Heart, Library of Tibet. Harper San Francisco, 1995. All other quotations of the Dalai Lama taken from interviews recorded by the author.

For many centuries, Ganden was the
light of Tibetan civilization. Methodically destroyed
during the cultural revolution, this monastery stands
as the symbol both of a silent persecution
and of the Tibetan people's will to survive.